I Think: Geography

U.S. REGIONS

by Sharon Coletti

© InspirEd Educators, Inc.   Atlanta, Georgia

** It is the goal of InspirEd Educators, Inc. to create instructional materials that are interesting, engaging, and challenging. Our student-centered approach incorporates both content and skills, placing particular emphasis on reading, writing, vocabulary development, and critical and creative thinking in the content areas.

Edited by Kendra Corr

Cover graphics by Sharon Coletti and Print1 Direct

Copyright © 2008 by InspirEd Educators, Inc.

ISBN # 978-1-933558-41-7

** FOR INDIVIDUAL TEACHER / PARENT USE **

Printed in the United States of America

Tips for Teaching with InspirEd Educators Units

- Before beginning the unit, take time to look through the Objectives and lessons. This will give you an idea of what to emphasize and offer ideas for extensions.

- Give your student(s) the Objective worksheet at the beginning of unit study. The Objectives serve as an outline of the content to be covered and provide a means to review information. Have the student(s) define terms as you go through the lessons and thoroughly answer the essential questions. You can check answers as you go along or wait and check all the Objectives upon completion as a test review. It is important that your student(s) have some opportunity to receive feedback on the responses, since they are the basis of assessments provided at the end of the unit.

- Read through each lesson's materials before beginning the lesson. This will help you better understand the concepts; decide when and how to present the vocabulary, and prepare the handouts you will need.

- "Terms to know" can be introduced at the beginning of lessons or reviewed at the end, unless specified otherwise. In a few lessons the intent is for the student(s) to discover the meanings of the terms. You will find that many are already familiar, especially if you use other InspirEd units. "Terms to know" are included in all of our units for vocabulary development.

- Look over what we have given you and use whatever you feel your student(s) need. Suggestions are sometimes offered for enrichment, but feel free to use any lesson as a jumping off point to pursue other related topics of interest.

- Our materials are intended to prompt discussion. Often students' answers vary, which is good, but it's important that they be able to justify their opinions and ideas. Let the discussion flow!

- Websites are suggested throughout the unit; for additional information and research sites refer to the Resource Section in the back of the unit.

- InspirEd Educators Units are all about thinking and creativity, so allow yourself the freedom to adapt the materials as you see fit. Our goal is to provide a springboard for you to jump from in your teaching and your student(s)' learning.

- ENJOY! We at InspirEd Educators truly believe that education should be enjoyable! We, therefore, do our best to make our lessons interesting and varied. We want you and your student(s) to have fun while they learn!

About InspirEd

InspirEd Educators was founded in 2000 by author Sharon Coletti. Originally offering only comprehensive curriculum binders for a variety of social studies disciplines, the company launched its line of mini-units, excerpted and adapted from our other units in 2008. These smaller, flexible resources are ideal for individual, small, or large group instruction. We hope you will find this unique, child-centered approach valuable and that we can serve you again in the near future.

If you are interested in other mini-unit offerings or are interested in one of our more comprehensive, in-depth studies, you can find information on our website at **www.inspirededucators.com**. The larger units include MANY additional lesson plans as well as differentiated tests or extensive test banks. Additional mini-units can also be found at **www.inspirededhomeschoolers.com**.

In all our units the lessons vary daily and include:

- Critical reading in the content area
- Writing Activities
- Critical and creative thinking
- Problem-solving
- Test-taking skills
- Primary source analyses
- Multiple perspectives
- Graphic analyses
- Fascinating readings
- Simulations
- Story-telling
- Use of technology
- Debates
- Plays
- Research
- Graphic organizers
- AND SO MUCH MORE!!!!!

Thank you for choosing our materials,
Sharon Coletti, Author and President
InspirEd Educators

TABLE OF CONTENTS

U.S. REGIONS OBJECTIVES

Define and be able to use these words:

- geography
- region
- landform
- physical map
- elevation
- tourism
- island
- population
- population density
- urban
- rural
- agriculture
- coast
- estuary
- erosion
- pollution
- drought
- piedmont
- delta
- continental shelf
- tidewater
- plateau
- sandbar
- barrier island
- dialect
- tributary
- border
- primary source
- mouth

- depth
- prairie
- trend
- produce
- port
- peninsula
- cargo
- raw materials
- desert
- basin
- range
- plain
- escarpment
- suburb
- environmental group
- dam
- illegal
- immigration
- continent
- rain shadow
- earthquake
- volcano
- tsunami
- map key
- map scale
- culture
- conservation
- language
- capital
- refuge

Fully answer these questions:

1. Explain what regions are and how they are decided on. Use the United States as an example.
2. Describe the geography of the Northeast.
3. Describe the geography of the Southeast.
4. Describe the geography of the Midwest.
5. Describe the geography of the Southwest.
6. Describe the geography of the West.
7. Explain some of the major problems faced in each U.S. region.

Define and be able to use these words:

Unit terms are defined in the lessons in which they are introduced.

Fully answer these questions:

1. *Regions define areas with common features, but the features can and do vary greatly. The U.S., for example, can be divided into regions based on physical features such as mountains, plains, river and lake basins; dry land or fertile, and so forth. It can also be divided culturally, historically, or simply for convenience, such as corporate regions.*

2. *Though its landforms differ somewhat, much of the Northeast Region is a densely populated megalopolis. A line of coastal cities stretches from Washington, D.C. north to Portland, Maine. Also, along the ragged coastline are many estuaries, which are home to countless animals and sea life.*

3. *The Southeast is dominated by the Appalachian Mountains and the plateau and piedmont that flank them. A wide coastal plain with large areas of wetlands lines the region protected by barrier islands. Today many large cities are expanding rapidly throughout the region.*

4. *The Mississippi River and its tributaries, a vast river system, spread across the Midwest before emptying into the Gulf of Mexico in the South. Much of the land in the Midwest is very rich and is known as the "nation's breadbasket." In the northern tier of the region are the Great Lakes. The lakes are home to many large cities and busy ports with ships transporting manufactured goods and farm products.*

5. *The Southwest is a hot, dry region, covered mostly with deserts and dry plains. Lack of water and a rapidly-growing population, which includes many illegal immigrants who cross the Rio Grande River from Mexico, pose problems for state and local governments there.*

6. *The West is the largest region in the United States. It has three great mountain ranges, the Rockies, the Sierras, and the Cascades, with a vast, dry interior. Situated in the Ring of Fire, the region has many earthquakes and some active volcanoes, particularly in the Hawaiian Islands. Alaska, huge and cold for most of the year, is the largest state.*

7. *Population growth is a particular challenge for the Southeast and Southwest, where most of the fastest-growing cities are, as America's population shifts from Northeastern and Midwestern cities southward. A rapidly-growing immigrant population poses challenges to the West, Southwest, and elsewhere. The Southwest, which is already dry, and the Southeast, which has been plagued by drought for years, are already having difficulty providing enough water for the people.*

   The Northeast and Southeast both deal with the loss of coastal land and destruction of natural habitats. The West, too, faces loss of usable land due to serious and prolonged dry conditions and fires. The Midwest, while not losing its valuable land, is shifting ownership of it from family farms to vast, corporate ventures whose chemicals may endanger both people and wildlife.

O'Regional Ideas

Springboard:
Students should read the "Regions" passage and answer the questions.
(Answers will vary by location but should make sense.)

Objective: The student will be able to name and describe the major physical geographic regions of the United States.

Materials:
Regions (Springboard handout)
The Physical U.S. (handout)
Slicing the Pie (handout or transparency)
Road Trip (handout)

Terms to know:
geography - study of the earth and its features
region - a geographic area with common features
landform - a natural feature of land (mountain, desert, etc.)
physical map - a map that shows natural features
elevation - height of the land

Procedure:

- After discussing the Springboard, explain that *the student(s) will be learning a lot more about regions in this lesson and in the rest of the unit*.
- Hand out the "The Physical U.S." map. Explain that *geographers often group places with like elevations and/or like physical features as "regions."* Have the student(s) study the physical map to draw and identify areas with similar types of landforms or differing elevations that they see.
- Have them share their solutions and explain why they divided the map and named the regions as they did. Point out that *different geographers can and do define regions differently, so there can be more than one correct answer*.
- Allow the student(s) to suggest other ways geographers could divide the map. *(Answers will vary.)* Show the answer page and explain the "official PHYSICAL geographic regions" using the explanations below the map.
- Hand out or display "Slicing the Pie." Explain that *when tourists plan to visit the U.S. and request information from the government, it sends them regional information. The regions are those shown on the map*. Have the student(s) answer the question at the bottom of the page. *(Answers may vary, but the states grouped together have similar history, culture, economy, some common physical features, etc..)* Explain that *this unit will be based on these five U.S. regions*.
- Give the student(s) the "Road Trip" handout. Have them use what they've learned about America's regions to create a "Road Trip" diary as directed. Depending upon time and student ability, you could have the student(s) estimate times from place to place or simply number entries. The Internet or other resources could be used to learn more about views along the way. Encourage your student(s) to be accurate but imaginative as well.
- Have the student(s) share the "Road Trip" diaries and discuss.

REGIONS

"Region" is a term often used in geography. It can mean different things at different times, but usually describes an area of land or water. The places in a region are grouped together for some reason. It can be a group of states such as the West. It can also be many countries, such as the Middle East, or it can be an area crossed by a physical feature that covers many states or countries like the Rocky Mountains, the Alps, or the Himalayas.

Regions are areas used in the study of geography. A region is an area with something in common. The land could be covered in mountains or desert. The people could all speak the same language or have the same religion. It could be an area where corn is grown or where people go to spend the winter. There are so many ways to define regions.

A region can be based on location like the South. It could be based on climate like the Arctic, or earthquakes like the Pacific Rim. It can be defined by farming or other human activities, like the Corn Belt or the Sun Belt. Companies and clubs divide areas into regions based mainly on where people live and work.

Countries, states, landforms, and even the earth can be put into regions in any number of ways. Often, one place is part of many regions and is even divided into regions itself.

DIRECTIONS: Think about the place where you live. Then name at least **TWO** different regions where your city, town, etc. could fit. Explain why you named the regions you did.

_____

_____

_____

_____

_____

_____

_____

_____

_____

_____

_____

THE PHYSICAL U.S.

Directions: Study the physical map of the United States, looking particularly for areas you think would have much the same elevation and/or landforms. Draw lines to show these areas and name or describe each below.

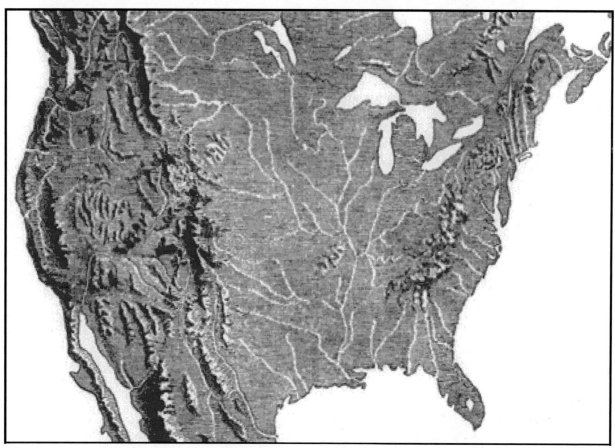

Courtesy of www.gutenberg.org/files/15884/15884-h/15884-h.htm

_____
_____
_____
_____
_____
_____
_____
_____
_____
_____
_____

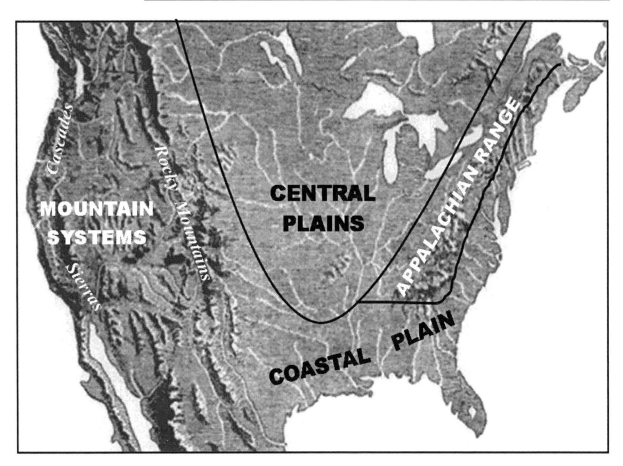

Answers may vary, but these are the regions often identified by geographers and are easy to see on the map.

Central Plains or Lowlands - *The area through the central U.S. to the Mississippi Valley is called the Central Plains or Interior Lowlands. This region includes the Great Plains, the prairies of the U.S. and Canada, the Great Lakes basin, and some of North America's major rivers.*

Mountain Systems - *The Rockies from northern Canada to New Mexico and the Pacific Ranges along the coast are part of a large region of Mountain Systems. The Appalachian Mountains in the east are sometimes considered part of this region, while other geographers identify them as a separate mountain system (Eastern Ranges and Western Ranges).*

Coastal Plains - *The Gulf-Atlantic Coastal Plain lies along the coasts of the Atlantic Ocean and Gulf of Mexico. This region has low elevation and is characterized by many coastal islands and inlets.*

Slicing the Pie

DIRECTIONS: There are many ways to divide the U.S. into regions, but this is the way this unit divides the nation. Study the map and lists of states to answer the question below.

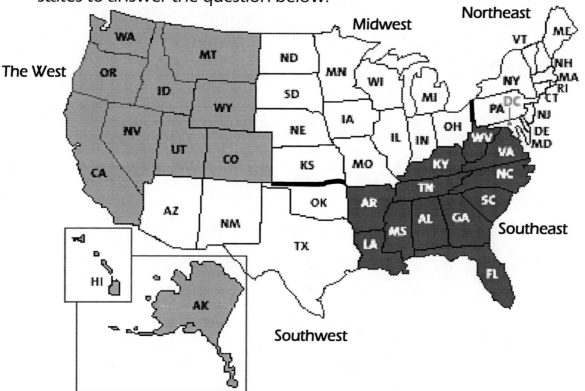

Northeast – Connecticut, Delaware, Maine, Maryland, Massachusetts, New Hampshire, New Jersey, New York, Pennsylvania, Rhode Island, Vermont, and Washington DC

Southeast – Alabama, Arkansas, Florida, Georgia, Kentucky, Louisiana, Mississippi, North Carolina, South Carolina, Tennessee, Virginia, and West Virginia

Midwest – Illinois, Iowa, Indiana, Kansas, Michigan, Minnesota, Missouri, Nebraska, North Dakota, Ohio, South Dakota, and Wisconsin

Southwest – Arizona, New Mexico, Oklahoma, and Texas

The West – Colorado, California, Idaho, Montana, Nevada, Oregon, Utah, Washington, Wyoming, Hawaii, and Alaska

? Why do you think the U.S. was divided in this way? List as many reasons as you can.

DIRECTIONS: What do you think it would be like to travel across the United States? Use what you've learned in this lesson and other information to write a travel "diary" about a road trip from one coast to the other. Use your imagination! Where you begin and end your "road trip" and who you meet is up to you. But you **MUST** use information about U.S. regions in your story.

_____

_____

_____

_____

_____

_____

_____

_____

_____

_____

_____

_____

_____

_____

_____

_____

_____

_____

_____

_____

_____

_____

_____

_____

_____

_____

_____

Pack Your Bags

Springboard:
Students should read "Northeast Tourism" and answer the questions.
(The first answer is "A. varied," based on the first sentence of the passage.
Other answers will vary, but students should explain their reasoning.)

Objective: The student will be familiar with the Northeastern states and be able to identify a few important geographic features of the region.

Materials: Northeast Tourism (Springboard handout)
                                              Postcards from Pennsylvania (handout)

Terms to know: **tourism** - travel for pleasure
                                              island - land with water all around it

Procedure:
- After discussing the Springboard, explain that *in this lesson the student(s) will be taking a short Internet field trip to (at least) one of the states in the Northeast Region*.
- Hand out copies of "Postcards from Pennsylvania." **For group instruction** assign or have the student(s) select one or more states as topics. Have them use the Internet or other resources to research tourism in their assigned states. **For individual instruction** have the student "visit" tourist sites around the region, sending postcards from each.
- Allow the student(s) time to read about their state's tourist sights, taking notes as needed. They should then write a postcard including pictures (drawn or printed out) for the state(s) researched.
- Have student(s) share their postcards, along with information about their states and discuss.

NORTHEAST TOURISM

Tourists who come to the Northeast can see many different sights. They can visit the region's big cities on the Northeast Corridor train. There is also great natural beauty to see.

The land of the region varies greatly, from the rocky coast of Maine to the rich farmlands of New Jersey and Pennsylvania. Hikers and skiers enjoy the mountains of the region. Most are part of the large Appalachian Range which runs from Vermont all the way to Georgia in the South. Mt. Washington in New Hampshire is the tallest mountain in the northeast and the windiest place in the whole United States!

Four important rivers pour into the Atlantic Ocean in the Northeast: the Delaware, the Hudson, the Connecticut, and the Kennebec. Islands line the coast from Massachusetts to Maryland. Cape Cod has Plymouth Rock and other tourist sites. Nantucket and Martha's Vineyard are home to many of the rich and famous. Long Island, Manhattan, and Staten Island are crowded with busy New Yorkers. Many people visit the giant Niagara Falls, which is also in New York. There is much to see and do in the Northeast.

Based on the reading, which word **BEST** describes the sights to see in the Northeast?

    A. varied

    B. important

    C. windy

    D. mountainous

Of the places in the reading, which one seems like it would be **MOST** interesting to you? Why? _____

_____

_____

_____

_____

_____

Postcards from Pennsylvania,

New York, New Jersey, Maryland, Delaware Connecticut, Rhode Island, Massachusetts, Vermont, New Hampshire, and Maine

DIRECTIONS: Find out enough about tourist sights in your state to make a postcard about it. The postcards should help others learn about your state. Be ready to share what you have learned.

Megalopolis

Objective: The student will be able to explain differences between urban and rural areas.

Materials: Megalopolis (Springboard handout)
                        Place-to-Place (handout)

Terms to know: **population** - the number of people in a place
                        population density - a measure of the number of people per square mile (or kilometer)
                        urban - having to do with cities
                        rural - having to do with the countryside
                        agriculture - farming

Procedure:

- In discussing the Springboard, explain that _an area is a megalopolis if it has high population density where large urban areas grow together_. (Review the first two terms and the fact that "urban areas have high population density.")
- Then point out that there are also areas of the Northeast that look completely black in the photograph. Explain that _while there are huge cities in the Northeast Region of the United States, there are still large rural areas as well_. Have the student(s) describe what they would expect to see in the rural areas *(farms, forests, mountains, small towns, etc.)*.
- Hand out copies of "Place-to-Place." Have the student(s) work individually or in pairs to list the pros and cons of urban and rural areas.
- Allow them to share their answers and discuss. *Possible answers include:*
  URBAN: *Positives include many and varied activities, more job opportunities, great shopping, greater diversity (reflected in interesting restaurants), opportunities for cultural experiences (plays, galleries, etc.), and more educational options (public, private, community schools, etc.). Negatives include crowded living conditions, higher crime rates, pollution, more stress, traffic, long lines, expensive housing, etc.*
  RURAL: *Positives include natural beauty, relaxed lifestyles, fresher foods, less crime, generally lower cost of housing, more open space for children to play, etc. Negatives include fewer options for activities, fewer jobs which often pay less, fewer cultural experiences, schools, restaurants, shopping, and so forth.)*

MEGALOPOLIS!!!

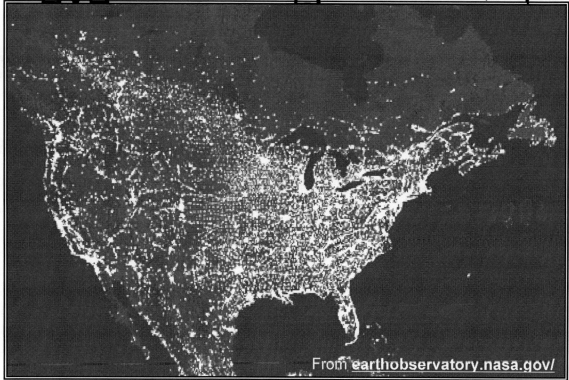

From earthobservatory.nasa.gov/

This night time picture from space shows that the Northeast Region of the United States has a large megalopolis more than 500 miles long. The northeast megalopolis stretches from Maine in the north all the way to Washington, DC in the south.

What do you think a "megalopolis" is? _____
_____
_____
_____
_____
_____

What do you think this "place" is like? _____
_____
_____
_____
_____
_____

PLACE-TO-PLACE

DIRECTIONS: List the good (+) and bad (-) points of URBAN and RURAL areas to compare the two kinds of places.

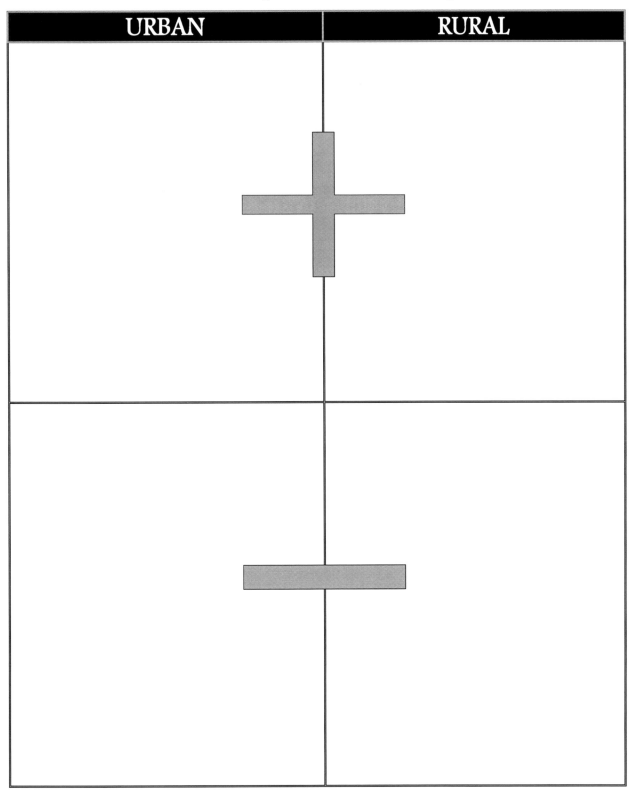

URBAN	RURAL

Crabs and Lawwwbstahs

Springboard:
Students should read "Very Important Estuaries"
and answer the questions.

Objective: The student will be able to explain what estuaries are, the kinds of economic activities that take place there, and problems facing America's estuaries.

Materials:
Very Important Estuaries (Springboard handout)
Waterman (handout or transparency)
Lobsterman (handout or transparency)
Tell a Tale; Spin a Yarn (handout)
Short Story Scoring (handout)

Terms to know:
coast - land next to an ocean
estuary - body of water with a mixture of fresh and salt water
erosion - wearing away of land on the earth
pollution - something that makes a place harmful or unfit for living things
drought - long period of time with below-normal rainfall

Procedure:
- After reviewing the Springboard, explain that *in this lesson the student(s) will learn more about the lives and jobs of some of the people who live and work in northeastern estuaries.*
- Hand out or display the "Waterman" and "Lobsterman" readings. Have your student(s) read the narratives and briefly discuss the ways the two workers are similar. *(Both men fish in estuaries, own their own boats, and face uncertainties, low yields, etc.)*
- Then hand out copies of "Tell a Tale; Spin a Yarn." Explain that *the student(s) will be writing their own stories about life in a northeastern estuary.* Review the directions and note taking categories. Students should then work individually to plan, write, and revise their stories. (**NOTE:** This can and ideally should be done as a cross-disciplinary activity with Language Arts.)
- As the student(s) begin the revision phase, hand out the "Short Story Scoring" form to use as a guide. When the stories are complete, they should evaluate their work.
- Allow time to share and discuss the stories.

VERY IMPORTANT ESTUARIES

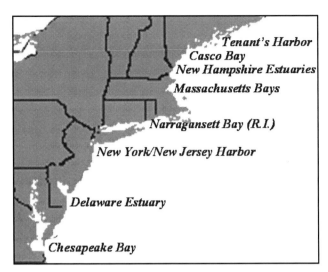

Tenant's Harbor
Casco Bay
New Hampshire Estuaries
Massachusetts Bays
Narragansett Bay (R.I.)
New York/New Jersey Harbor
Delaware Estuary
Chesapeake Bay

Estuaries are partly closed-in areas of water along coastlines. The water in estuaries is a mix of fresh water flowing to the sea and salt water from the ocean. The northeast coast of the United States has many estuaries. All are rich in plant and animal life.

Shore birds, mammals, fish, lobster, crab, and other shellfish are just some of the animals that live in estuaries. Birds flying north or south often stop in estuaries to rest and eat. Many kinds of fish and shellfish lay their eggs there.

Estuaries are also good for people. Visitors come to estuaries for their beauty. Boating, fishing, swimming, and bird watching are some of the activities that can be enjoyed there. Tourism and fishing provide many jobs for people in estuary areas. Scientists and geographers study estuaries and how they change.

Sadly, many estuaries are changing because of humans and storms. Beach homes and shops have taken over land. Water and air in estuaries are becoming polluted. Beaches are wearing away due to hurricanes and other storms. Some steps are now being taken to help save America's estuaries. They are too important to lose!

Another name for an estuary is
    A. an activity.
    B. a river.
    C. an ocean.
    D. a bay.

Estuaries help people living nearby by
    A. bringing money to the area.
    B. offering rest to flying birds.
    C. being places to build houses.
    D. mixing fresh and salt water.

The reading says all of these are problems in America's estuaries, **EXCEPT**
    A. erosion.
    B. building.
    C. tourism.
    D. pollution.

VERY IMPORTANT ESTUARIES
ANSWERS & EXPLANATIONS

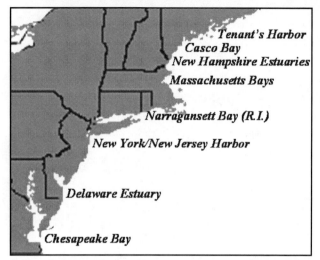

Tenant's Harbor
Casco Bay
New Hampshire Estuaries
Massachusetts Bays
Narragansett Bay (R.I.)
New York/New Jersey Harbor
Delaware Estuary
Chesapeake Bay

Estuaries are partly closed-in areas of water along coastlines. The water in estuaries is a mix of fresh water flowing to the sea and salt water from the ocean. The northeast coast of the United States has many estuaries. All are rich in plant and animal life.

Shore birds, mammals, fish, lobster, crab, and other shellfish are just some of the animals that live in estuaries. Birds flying north or south often stop in estuaries to rest and eat. Many kinds of fish and shellfish lay their eggs there.

Estuaries are also good for people. Visitors come to estuaries for their beauty. Boating, fishing, swimming, and bird watching are some of the activities that can be enjoyed there. Tourism and fishing provide many jobs for people in estuary areas. Scientists and geographers study estuaries and how they change.

Sadly, many estuaries are changing because of humans and storms. Beach homes and shops have taken over land. Water and air in estuaries are becoming polluted. Beaches are wearing away due to hurricanes and other storms. Some steps are now being taken to help save America's estuaries. They are too important to lose!

Another name for an estuary is

    A. an activity.   C. an ocean.

    B. a river.   D. a bay. *

(Students should always look at maps and pictures for information. The map of northeastern estuaries shows three different ones called "bays.")

Estuaries help people living nearby by

    A. bringing money to the area. *

    B. offering rest to flying birds.

    C. being places to build houses.

    D. mixing fresh and salt water.

(Choices B-D are not helpful to people, though many houses are built there. A is a better choice since "tourism and fishing provide many jobs.")

The reading says all of these are problems in America's estuaries, **EXCEPT**

    A. erosion.

    B. building.

    C. tourism. *

    D. pollution.

(Tourism is identified as a source of jobs, while the other three choices are mentioned as changes brought by humans and storms.)

Waterman

My name's Hank. I'm a waterman in the Chesapeake Bay. I've been fishing for crab and other shellfish here nearly my whole life. Fishing is big business in Maryland where I live. People come from all over to our crab houses. Tables are covered in brown paper and crabs are piled up on top. It's quite a sight to see — and something to taste, too.

Men like me go to work on skipjacks. This is a picture of my boat. I'm lucky in that I own my own fishing company. It's good because I'm my own boss. It's bad though when the catch is short.

Water pollution and over-fishing have hurt the business. That's not even counting the droughts we've had in the past few years. There used to be tons of crab out there, but now we have had some bad years.

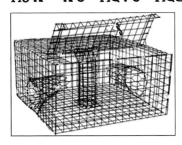

Me and other watermen put out the crab pots. That's what we call the traps. You can see what a crab pot looks like in the picture. We just set out a bunch of crab pots and leave them. After a time crabs crawl inside for the bait we put in there. Once a crab gets in, he can't get out again.

I pull in different things in my pots, but my favorite catch by a long shot is blue crab. It just so happens to be my favorite thing to eat, too. If you've never eaten a blue crab, you should! It might look like a big, mean critter, but it's the sweetest thing in the whole wide world!

Lobsterman

I'm Robert and I live in Tenant's Harbor, Maine. I'm what you call a lobsterman because I catch lobsters for a living. Some think what I do may be a bit foolish and sometimes dangerous, but I love it.

I've even got my own boat. I named her "Chasin' Tail." If you've ever eaten a lobster, you know why. The tail's the best part. It's just wonderful!

Owning my own business is great, too. I like being my own boss after years of working for somebody else. Still, it can be scary. Storms can hurt the boat and even hurt me, too. And if the catch is down, I take all the losses for gas and other costs. It sure can make for a hard life at times.

The way to catch lobsters is to put out creels with bait in them. Creels are traps like the one in the picture. I put out a bunch of creels with floats coming off them. Then after a time I go back and get them. Since I run a small boat, I pull the creels in by hand. Bigger boats have machines to do it.

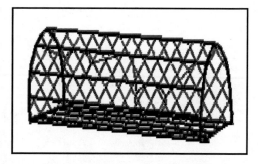

You have to be really careful getting the lobster out. They'll snap your fingers off with their claws if you don't watch out!

Tell a Tale, Spin a Yarn

DIRECTIONS: Use what you learned about estuaries and fishing to write a short story. It can be about a made-up person, or you can write about yourself. Use this form to help plan your tale. Be sure to use facts from the readings in your yarn.

Where does the story take place? Describe the place.	
Who are the people in the story? Tell about each.	
What problem do the people face?	
How does the problem work out in the end? (It can have a happy or sad ending.)	

SHORT STORY SCORING

Name _____

Story Name _____

Rate each point from 1 to 4 and then your teacher will score the story, too:

1= Poor	2 = Fair	3 = Good	4 = Excellent
		Student	Teacher

	Student	Teacher
Describes setting	_____	_____
Describes people	_____	_____
Clear problem	_____	_____
Works out problem	_____	_____
Uses facts as details	_____	_____
Uses writing skills	_____	_____

Total Score / Grade:

SHORT STORY SCORING

Name _____

Story Name _____

Rate each point from 1 to 4 and then your teacher will score the story, too:

1= Poor	2 = Fair	3 = Good	4 = Excellent
		Student	Teacher

	Student	Teacher
Describes setting	_____	_____
Describes people	_____	_____
Clear problem	_____	_____
Works out problem	_____	_____
Uses facts as details	_____	_____
Uses writing skills	_____	_____

Total Score / Grade:

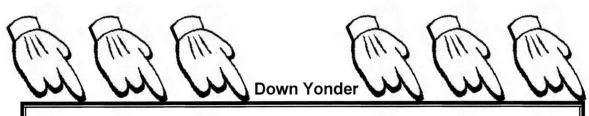

Down Yonder

Objective: The student will be able to identify some important physical features of the Southeast Region.

Materials: Geography of the Southeast Region (Springboard handout)
Exploring the Southeast (handout)

Terms to know: **piedmont** - rolling land at the foot of a mountain range
delta - triangle of land at the mouth of a river
continental shelf - underwater land that slopes from the land into the deeper ocean
tidewater - low coastal land drained by streams that rise and fall with the tides
plateau - high, flat tableland

Procedure:

- After discussing the Springboard, explain that *in this lesson the student(s) will learn more about the Southeast's important geographic features*.
- Hand out copies of "Exploring the Southeast." Student(s) should work individually, in pairs, or small groups to locate information on the Internet or in other resources to complete the scavenger hunt.
- Have the student(s) share their answers and discuss, adding information to their descriptions as appropriate. During the discussion have them point out some similar geographic features found among the southeastern states. *(Many of the states have mountains, piedmont, coastal plains, etc.)* If not mentioned, point out that *the coastal states also share similar features such as wetlands, offshore islands, and estuaries*.

Geography of the Southeast Region

DIRECTIONS: Study the two maps and list as many facts as you can find about the physical geography of the Southeast.

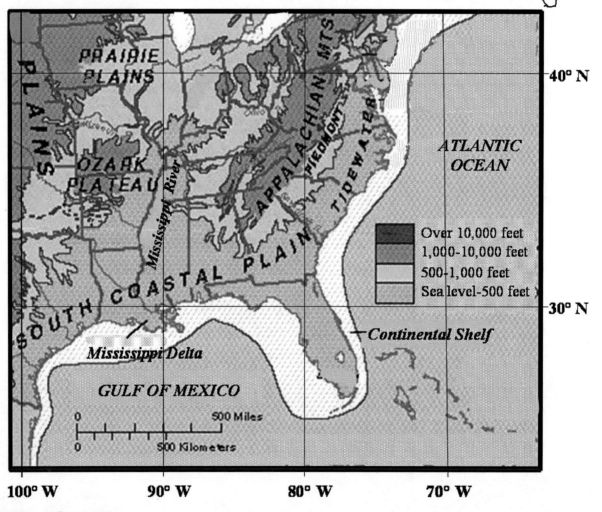

THINK ABOUT... Location, size, regions, rivers, mountains, bodies of water, etc. _____

_____

_____

_____

# Exploring the Southeast

DIRECTIONS: Use the Internet and other sources to "visit" each place and take notes. Jot down what you think is important about each. Pictures are good too.

Appalachian Mountains -

Ozarks -

Coastal Plain -

Fall Line -

Mississippi River -

Tidewater (Low Country) -

Everglades -

DIRECTIONS: Use the Internet and other sources to "visit" each place and take notes. Jot down what you think is important about each. Pictures are good too.

Appalachian Mountains - *The Appalachian Mountains are about 1,500 miles long, stretching from central Alabama and Georgia up through the New England states and into northeastern Canada. The Appalachian Trail extends through most of the range. Some smaller mountain ranges included in the Appalachians are the Cumberland Mts. in Tennessee, the Great Smokey Mts. in Tennessee and North Carolina, and the Blue Ridge Mts. in Virginia. The range's highest point is Mt. Mitchell in North Carolina at more than 6,500 ft.*

Ozarks - *Locally referred to as mountains, the Ozarks are actually a large plateau extending across the northern half of Arkansas and into Oklahoma and Missouri. The Ozarks were "mountains" at one time but have been flattened by erosion over time.*

Coastal Plain - *This area of the southern and southeastern U.S. extends to the continental shelf and has mostly flat land with forests. Areas along the coasts include bayous, deltas, marshes, mud fluts, and swamps. There are also many barrier islands with wetlands.*

Fall Line - *The fall line is the area where a mountain region and a coastal plain meet. The fall line is most easily seen where a river crosses it, since there will usually be large rapids or waterfalls. There are many waterfalls in the southeastern U.S.*

Mississippi River - *The Mississippi ranks third in length and second in area among the world's rivers. It is the largest river in North America, flowing from its source in Minnesota, through the middle of the U.S. to the Louisiana delta and into the Gulf of Mexico. The Mississippi River Basin includes all or part of 31 states, covering about 40% of the U.S. and about 1/8 of North America.*

Tidewater (Low Country) - *The Tidewater is the area along the coast that is very close to sea level. It's located in Virginia, North Carolina, and South Carolina (where it is called the Low Country). This region also has many wetlands, which is where water covers the land.*

Everglades - *Stretching south from the 700 square-mile Lake Okeechobee, the Everglades is a wide, slow-moving river of marsh and saw grass covering some 4,500 square miles, which flows quietly towards the estuaries of the Gulf of Mexico. The swampy Everglades is a vast ecosystem that supports a wide array of animal and plant life.*

Protective Shield

Objective: The student will be able to explain what barrier islands are, how they grow and change, and the impact humans can have on them.

Materials: Atlantic Hurricanes (Springboard handout)
                      On Guard!? (transparency or handouts)
                      Island Planning Project (handouts)

Terms to know: **sandbar** - raised area of land built up under the water along coasts
                      barrier island - a long, narrow island along the coast that protects the mainland from heavy waves and tides

Procedure:

- After discussing the Springboard, explain that *there are many offshore islands (like Roanoke off the southeast and Gulf coasts of the U.S.) called "barrier islands."* (Review the definition.) Go on to explain that *although Roanoke Island did not prove to be a good place for early settlers to live, barrier islands are actually wonderful and important places*.

- Display or distribute "On Guard!?" Read together or have the student(s) read the information by themselves. Point out that *the map shows North Carolina's barrier islands, the Outer Banks, but similar barrier islands line much of the southeastern coastline*.

- Then hand out the "Island Planning Project" guide. The student(s) may work in "planning groups" or as "individual consultants" to decide what should be done with one barrier island they select (or are assigned). A search for "barrier islands (state)" nets many possibilities.

- The student(s) should briefly research their island to learn about its existing condition. *(Is it already built up or is it mostly in its natural state? Is the island populated by poor people who could use jobs and income? Has it become a playground for the rich? Is the Planning Group trying to control or encourage growth?)* They should then make decisions to complete the "Island Planning Group" form.

- Have the student(s) describe their island and explain the decisions they made.

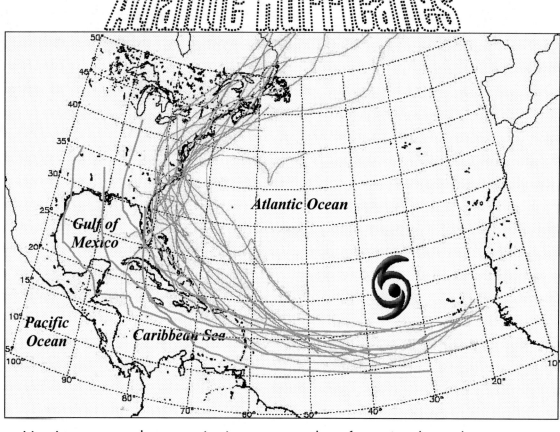

Hurricanes are huge, spinning storms that form in the Atlantic Ocean, Caribbean Sea, Gulf of Mexico, and in the eastern Pacific Ocean. Atlantic hurricanes are the ones that usually hit the United States. Most form during hurricane season which lasts from June 1st to November 30th.

Hurricanes have high winds of at least 74 miles per hour and heavy rain. The wind and rain spins around an "eye." When they hit land, the rain, strong winds, and giant waves can cause terrible damage. The heavy waves, called the storm surge, are very dangerous! The storm surge is the biggest reason to get away from the coast during a hurricane.

Based on the map, **MOST** of the Atlantic hurricanes hit the U.S.

    A. in the Caribbean Sea   C. along the southeastern coast.

    B. along the Gulf coast.   D. in the North Atlantic Ocean.

What kind of "terrible damage" can these hurricanes cause? _____

_____

_____

_____

_____

_____

on Guard!?

North Carolina Coast and Barrier Islands

Atlantic Ocean

Barrier islands are narrow islands off coastlines. They help protect the mainland from waves and storms. Barrier islands are formed by both the land and the sea. Sand and soil is washed from mountains into streams and down rivers into the sea. Once there, tides push the soil to form sandbars and islands.

Barrier islands build up over time. Birds bring seeds, eggs, and insects to live on growing islands. Some animals such as snakes and turtles swim to the islands. Others may wash ashore in floods or, like horses, cats, and others, be brought to the islands by humans. Over time, barrier islands become full of life and a wonder to see. Their beauty brings people who build homes and towns. Tourists come to enjoy the views and peaceful atmosphere.

Today, many of the barrier islands in the southeast and other places are filled with hotels and shops. Tourists come to sun, swim, and play games. Many people earn their incomes from the building and tourism, but what happens to the islands?

Too many people can be bad for barrier islands. Buildings take up space that animals use to nest. Sea turtles nest on barrier islands all around the Southeast. Yet as homes, hotels, and roads fill the islands' shores, there is less land left for the turtles.

Barrier islands also protect the estuaries and wetlands behind them. The estuaries offer nesting places to thousands of creatures. The question is how well barrier islands protect the other lands.

These islands are counted on to block storms and high seas. Sometimes though, the island may not be able to hold back the ocean. Every year people on barrier islands lose homes, stores, and land. They file claims to pay for damage. Companies or the government often foot the bill for the losses. So, is it fair for these people to rebuild?

More land is likely to be lost. One problem is that people do not understand how barrier islands work. The islands do protect the mainland, but they are always changing. Storms may wash away part of one island and move the sand to another. Of course the change is slow. It happens over time, but it is always taking place.

Island Planning Project

DIRECTIONS: You were picked to be part of a barrier island planning project. Your island has been named as one of the most beautiful places in the Southeast. Research your island to decide if, and / or how, you want your island to grow and develop.

Background – Describe the island you are planning for.

_____

_____

_____

_____

_____

1. What, if anything, do you think should be built on your island? Explain.

_____

_____

_____

_____

_____

2. What do you think needs to be done about the island's plant and animal life? Explain.

_____

_____

_____

_____

3. Is there anything else you think needs to be done about the island?

_____

_____

_____

_____

Springboard:
Students should read "Southern Dialect" and answer the questions.
(Except for the first question, defined below, answers will vary.)

Objective: The student will be able to explain the urban and rural make-up of the Southeast.

Materials:
Southern Dialect (Springboard handout)
Rural? or Urban? (handout)
What Does This Map Show? (handout or transparency)
Pick A City (handout)

Terms to know:
dialect - a regional form of a language

Procedure:

· In discussing the Springboard, explain that *while some people throughout the Southeast states may use some or all of the words, phrases, and pronunciations in the Springboard, many do not. In fact many people who live in the region moved there from other parts of the country or other countries in the world.*

· Distribute "Rural? or Urban?" and have the student(s) complete the handout. *(Nearly ¾ of the people in the Southeast live in cities. Over 1/3 of the largest 100 U.S. cities are in the South. Many of the fastest-growing urban areas are in the South.)*

· Hand out or display "What Does This Map Show?" and have the student(s) answer the question *(population density).* Have the student(s) point out the most populated areas *(darkest on the map).* Point out that *large areas of the Southeast are colored in light grey.* Have the student(s) explain what that means and the types of activities that most likely go on in those areas. *(These are rural areas with very small towns. Activities likely include agriculture, timber and/or wetlands.)* Ask student(s) why they think there are so many big cities in the region. *(The Southeast is one of the fastest-growing regions in the country. The good climate attracts people and companies so there are many different kinds of jobs. Some people are transferred to southern cities because many large companies have offices there.)*

 · Hand out copies of the "Pick A City" note taking form. Have your student(s) work individually or in pairs to pick a city from the "Of the Largest 100 American Cities" chart (or you can assign). They should use the Internet or other resources to find information about that city and what it offers to people who live there and/or visitors. They should then create a brochure to attract people to the city, either for business, tourism, or to live.

· Have the student(s) share their city information and brochures and discuss.

Southern Dialect

Hey Y'all!

hey - hello
y'all - you
ah - eye
agin - again
aink pin - pen
all y'all - everybody
aways – far
bald - boiled
bar - bear
beal - bill
britches - pants
caint - cannot
carry - bring; take
chayer - chair
chesta drawers - dresser
chunk - throw
crine - weeping
cut off - turn off
dinner - noon meal
drawed up - shrunk
far - fire

favor - look like
fixin' to - going to
fixins – trimmings
fret - pout
get shed of - get rid of
gitgo - beginning
got hold - got
got a notion - thinking of
greens - turnips or collards
grits - cooked ground corn
hanker - want
hep – help
havin' a hissy fit - angry
holt - hold
I reckon - I guess so
intar - whole
Jever - Did you ever?
kin - family
left off - dropped off
liddle biddy - small
mah - my

mind - obey
parts – neighborhood
prit near - close to
probly - probably
reckon - believe
recollect - remember
rilly - really
roont - ruined
sayud - sad, said
set - sit
show - movie
sleepers - pajamas
Son - male (talking to)
stoop - porch; front step
story - lie
sweet tea - iced tea
tote - carry
upchuck – throw up
wash cloth - rag
yale - yell
yonder – there

1. What do you think a "dialect" is?

2. Is there a dialect in the area where you live?

3. Would you say that most people in an area speak the dialect there?

JUST FOR FUN: Practice having a conversation in southern dialect.

% of Population by Area

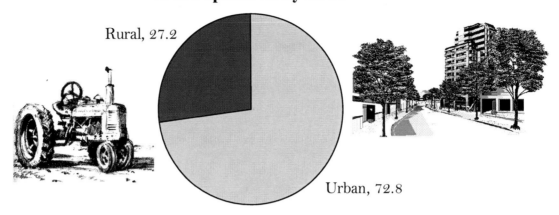

Rural, 27.2

Urban, 72.8

OF THE LARGEST 100 AMERICAN CITIES... (Based on 2000 U.S. Census Data)

METROPOLITAN AREA	RANKS	METROPOLITAN AREA	RANKS
Atlanta, GA	11	Knoxville, TN	62
Miami-Fort Lauderdale, FL	12	Baton Rouge, LA	69
Tampa-St. Petersburg, FL	20	Sarasota-Bradenton, FL	72
Orlando, FL	27	Little Rock, AR	73
Norfolk-Virginia Beach, VA	30	Charleston, SC	76
Charlotte-Gastonia, NC	33	Mobile, AL	78
New Orleans, LA	34	Columbia, SC	79
Greensboro-Winston Salem, NC	36	Daytona Beach, FL	82
Nashville, TN	38	Lakeland-Winter Haven, FL	83
Raleigh-Durham, NC	40	Johnson City, TN-Kingsport, VA	84
Memphis, TN	43	Lexington, KY	85
West Palm Beach-Boca Raton, FL	44	Augusta-Aiken, GA-SC	86
Jacksonville, FL	45	Melbourne-Titusville, FL	87
Louisville, KY	49	Chattanooga, TN	89
Richmond-Petersburg, VA	50	Fort Myers, FL	94
Greenville-Spartanburg, SC	51	Jackson, MS	95
Birmingham, AL	54	Pensacola, FL	99

DIRECTIONS: Write at least TWO sentences to describe the Southeast Region based on information in the graph and chart.

_____

_____

_____

_____

_____

_____

_____

_____

What Does This Map Show?

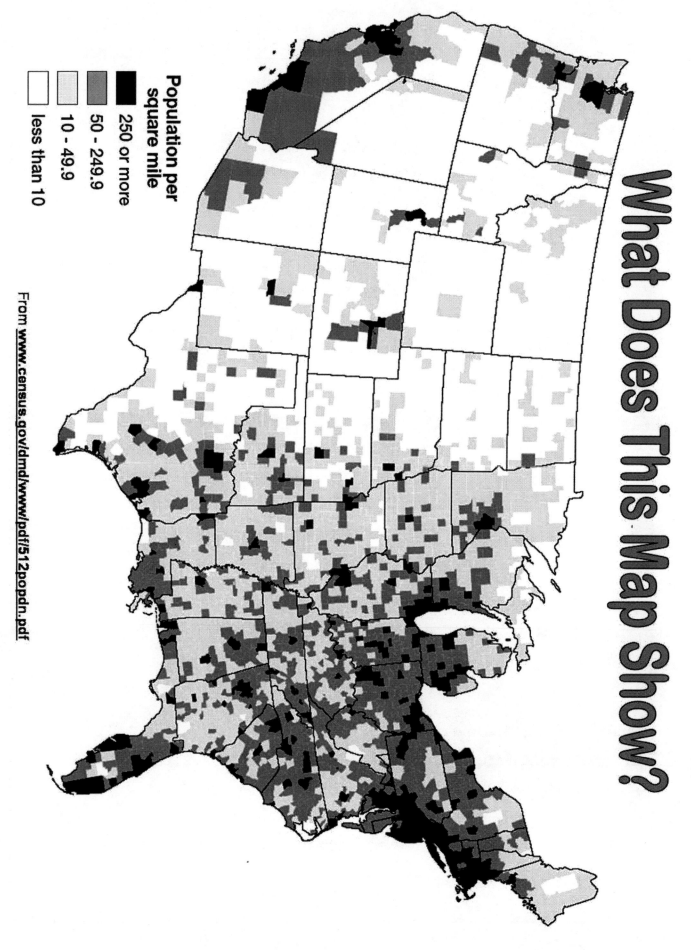

Population per square mile

- **250 or more**
- 50 – 249.9
- 10 – 49.9
- less than 10

From www.census.gov/dmd/www/pdf/512popdn.pdf

Pick A City

Physical Geography:

Cultural Characteristics:

Things to see and do:

The Mighty Mississip'

Springboard:
Students should study "The Mississippi and Its Tributaries" map
and answer the questions.

Objective: The student will be able to explain the importance of the Mississippi River and its tributaries.

Materials:	The Mississippi and Its Tributaries (Springboard handout) From Life on the Mississippi by Mark Twain (handout) Understanding Primary Sources (handout)
Terms to know:	**tributary** - a river that flows into a larger river **border** - line dividing two countries, states, etc. **primary source** - writings from a time period (letters, diaries, books, newspapers, etc.) **mouth** - place where a river empties into an ocean or other large body of water **depth** - measure of how deep water is

Procedure:

- After reviewing the Springboard, explain that *the Mississippi River and its tributaries flow southward to the Gulf of Mexico from the region known as the Midwest.* Go on to explain that *the writer Mark Twain knew the Mississippi River well from growing up and working on it. In this lesson the student(s) will read a primary source (review definition) by Mark Twain from his book about the river.*

- Hand out "From Life on the Mississippi by Mark Twain." Depending upon student ability, read the passage together or have the student(s) read it independently and summarize what they learned from it.

- Then distribute "Understanding Primary Sources" and have the student(s) complete it using the excerpt from Twain's book as the primary source.

- Have the student(s) share answers and discuss. *(Answers may vary.)* During the discussion have student(s) explain why the Mississippi River is so important. *(Goods are shipped into and out of states in the country's midsection; it is a major trade route with major port cities; the land around it is fertile and good for farming, it provides water, etc.)*

The Mississippi and Its Tributaries

The Mississippi River flows from
- A. Mississippi to Wisconsin.
- B. Colorado into Arkansas.
- C. Minnesota to Louisiana.
- D. Iowa through Kentucky.

The Mississippi River forms the border between
- A. Minnesota and Nebraska.
- B. North and South Dakota.
- C. Kentucky and Indiana.
- D. Illinois and Missouri.

The Arkansas, Missouri, and Ohio Rivers all flow
- A. from west to east.
- B. into the Mississippi.
- C. to the Gulf of Mexico.
- D. northeast to southwest.

Based on the map, what is a "tributary"?

The Mississippi and Its Tributaries Answers and Explanations

The Mississippi River flows from
  A. Mississippi to Wisconsin.
  B. Colorado into Arkansas.
  C. Minnesota to Louisiana. *
  D. Iowa through Kentucky.

(Rivers always flow into a body of water, and students have already learned that the Mississippi flows into the Gulf of Mexico in Louisiana.)

The Mississippi River forms the border between
  A. Minnesota and Nebraska.
  B. North and South Dakota.
  C. Kentucky and Indiana.
  D. Illinois and Missouri. *

(If students are unsure about the meaning of "border," the term should be explained at this opportunity.)

The Arkansas, Missouri, and Ohio Rivers all flow
  A. from west to east.
  B. into the Mississippi. *
  C. to the Gulf of Mexico.
  D. northeast to southwest.

(If students understand the first question, they should recognize this.)

Based on the map, what is a "tributary"? *It is a river flowing into a larger river.*

From <u>Life on the Mississippi</u> by Mark Twain, 1863

CHAPTER 1

"The Mississippi is well worth reading about. It is not a commonplace river, but on the contrary is in all ways remarkable. Considering the Missouri its main branch, it is the longest river in the world -- four thousand three hundred miles. It seems safe to say that it is also the crookedest river in the world, since in one part of its journey it uses up one thousand three hundred miles to cover the same ground that the crow would fly over in six hundred and seventy-five. ... No other river has so vast a drainage-basin: it draws its water supply from twenty-eight States and Territories; from Delaware, on the Atlantic seaboard, and from all the country between that and Idaho on the Pacific slope -- a spread of forty-five degrees of longitude. The Mississippi receives and carries to the Gulf water from fifty-four rivers that are

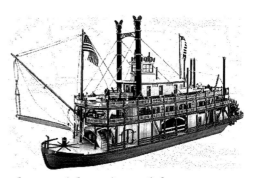

navigable by steamboats (above), and from some hundreds that are navigable by flats and keels (left).

The area of its drainage-basin is as great as the combined areas of England, Scotland, Wales, Ireland, France, Germany, Austria, Italy, Spain, Portugal, and Turkey (right); almost all this wide region is fertile...

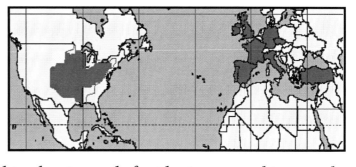

It is a remarkable river in this: that instead of widening toward its mouth, it grows narrower; grows narrower and deeper. From the ... Ohio to a point half way down to the sea, the width averages a mile in high water: thence to the sea the width steadily diminishes (gets smaller), until, above the mouth, it is but little over half a mile. At the ... Ohio the Mississippi's depth is eighty-seven feet; the depth increases gradually, reaching one hundred and twenty-nine just above the mouth... Although the Mississippi's mud builds land but slowly, down at the mouth ... it builds fast enough in better protected regions higher up: for instance, Prophet's Island ... the river has added seven hundred acres to it..."

Understanding Primary Sources

DIRECTIONS: Primary sources can be hard to understand because they use "old time" or hard-to-read words. It can help if you take time to think through the primary source and why it was written.

1. What kind of primary source is it? _____

2. Date of the source: _____

3. Author (or creator): _____

4. Why do you think the author wrote (or the creator made) this source?

   _____

   _____

   _____

5. Who did the author (creator) think would see or read the source?

   _____

   _____

   _____

6. List FIVE things from the source that you think are important:

   _____

   _____

   _____

   _____

   _____

7. Write at least TWO questions you would ask the author (or creator) if you could. _____

   _____

   _____

   _____

   _____

Springboard:
Students should read "Prairie Lands" and
answer the questions.

Objective: The student will be able to explain how and why people moved into the central prairies of the United States and to describe their lifestyle.

Materials: Prairie Lands (Springboard handout)
America's Farms (handout)
Two Sides of the Coin (handout)
Weigh in on the Matter (handout)

Terms to know: **prairie** - grassland
trend - the way something is generally going
produce - farm products; fruits and vegetables

Procedure:
· After reviewing the Springboard, explain that *much of the area in the nation's midsection that was once covered in grasslands was devoted to agriculture; growing corn, wheat, and other grains. Now that area known as "America's Breadbasket" is changing once more*.
· Distribute "America's Farms" and have the student(s) study the graph and chart to answer the questions.
· Have the student(s) share their answers and discuss. *(Answers may vary. Many small farmers have lost their land as larger business farms have grown. Another reason is the growth of cities. Though data was not available by state beyond 1997, it's clear from the top graph that the number of farms has declined.)*
· Hand out copies of "Two Sides of the Coin" and "Weigh in on the Matter" and explain that *the rest of this lesson looks more closely at American agriculture, what is happening to it, and what its future holds*.
· Have the student(s) work individually, in pairs, or small groups to read the two viewpoints about farming. Then have them mark X's along the continuum for each question on the "Weigh in on the Matter" handout to express their views.
· Have the student(s) share their views and reasoning and discuss.

Prairie Lands

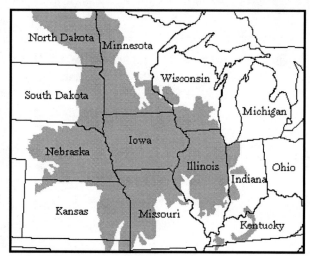

Prairies or grasslands once covered most of the central U.S. When the first white settlers moved to the area in the late 1700's, they found what looked like a vast sea of grass. The wind made the grass look like waves.

The first settlers on the prairie were likely soldiers of the American Revolution. Troops from that war and others were promised land for their efforts. Almost any soldier who wanted it could get 160 acres of land. Many soldiers took the offer and moved to the prairie.

By the early 1800's there was a mad dash to settle the region. People crossed the Mississippi and Ohio Rivers any way they could. Much of the prairie was settled by "squatters." Squatters worked the land, built houses, planted crops, and grazed cattle. Yet they had no real claim to their land. Some squatters had land they were living on sold out from under them. Finally, the government allowed people who settled land to buy it for $1.25 an acre.

All of these states had prairie land EXCEPT
    A. Minnesota.   C. Wisconsin.
    B. Nebraska.   D. Michigan.

Some land in the central U.S. was ___ by ___.
    A. bought ... squatters
    B. moved ... soldiers
    C. built ... land claims
    D. settled ... cattle

What would most likely **NOT** have been on the prairie in the 1800's?
    A. houses   B. trees   C. animals   D. crops

Prairie Lands
Answers & Explanations

Prairies or grasslands once covered most of the central U.S. When the first white settlers moved to the area in the late 1700's, they found what looked like a vast sea of grass. The wind made the grass look like waves.

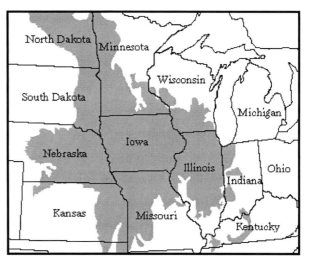

The first settlers on the prairie were likely soldiers of the American Revolution. Troops from that war and others were promised land for their efforts. Almost any soldier who wanted it could get 160 acres of land. Many soldiers took the offer and moved to the prairie.

By the early 1800's there was a mad dash to settle the region. People crossed the Mississippi and Ohio Rivers any way they could. Much of the prairie was settled by "squatters." Squatters worked the land, built houses, planted crops, and grazed cattle. Yet they had no real claim to their land. Some squatters had land they were living on sold out from under them. Finally, the government allowed people who settled land to buy it for $1.25 an acre.

All of these states had prairie land **<u>EXCEPT</u>**
    A. Minnesota.   C. Wisconsin.
    B. Nebraska.   D. Michigan. *
    (Even though it isn't labeled, students can conclude that the map relates to the passage information.)

Some land in the central U.S. was ___ by ___.   *(It is legitimate to*
    A. bought ... squatters *   *conclude that some*
    B. moved ... soldiers   *squatters bought*
    C. built ... land claims   *their land given*
    D. settled ... cattle   *the opportunity.)*

What would most likely **<u>NOT</u>** have been on the prairie in the 1800's?
    A. houses   B. trees *   C. animals   D. crops
    (As described, the prairies were "seas of grass." Houses, trees, and crops came with the settlers. Trees may have been planted but were not mentioned.)

America's Farms

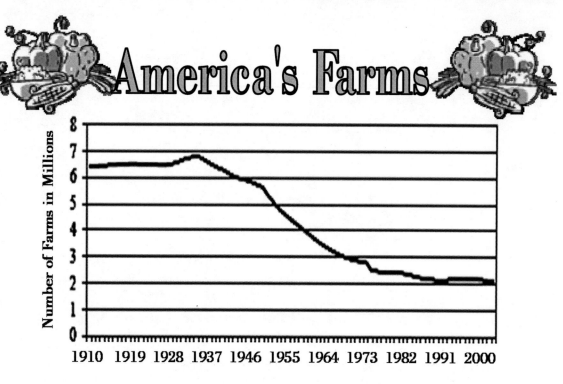

Number of Farms in Midwest Region by State

	1964	1978	1997
Illinois	132,822	104,690	73,051
Indiana	108,082	82,483	57,916
Iowa	154,162	121,339	90,792
Kansas	94,440	74,171	61,593
Michigan	93,504	60,426	40,027
Minnesota	131,163	98,671	73,367
Missouri	147,315	114,963	98,860
Nebraska	80,163	63,768	51,454
North Dakota	48,836	40,357	30,504
Ohio	120,381	86,934	68,591
South Dakota	49,703	38,741	31,284
Wisconsin	118,816	86,505	65,602

What do you think is the reason for the trend shown in the graph and the chart? _____

_____

_____

_____

What do you think has happened to the number of farms in the Midwest since 1997? _____

_____

TWO SIDES OF THE COIN

America is losing its small farms. This problem is at its worst in the Midwest. Every day small farmers lose their land to banks or have to sell their farms to big companies. The number of farms in the United States is less than half of what it was in the mid 1900's. So why does this matter?

Small farms are very important to rural America. As large farms take the place of smaller ones, rural towns are also lost. Shops, schools, and other places close. People lose their jobs and their homes.

Small farms are important to the nation too. Often small farmers raise both crops and animals. Each year they change which fields they use for each. Animals keep their land fertile. This means farmers do not have to use as many harmful chemicals. Small farms pollute less than large ones.

Small farmers care about the country. The Midwest is called "America's Heartland" for a good reason. Small farmers care about the land and the people who will be eating their food.

Big business has shown over and over that the only thing it cares about is money. Companies care less about what is good for the earth and the people on it than they do about their incomes.

The U.S. is losing its small farms to big companies for a reason. The country is bigger and needs more food for its people. Company farms can grow more food at lower costs than small farms.

One way they do this is by focusing on just one thing. The companies can spend the money to buy the best machines to use for that farm product.

They also pay large sums to study the crop or animal. Companies are always looking for new ways to grow more and better produce at a lower cost.

Large companies that own farms often own other businesses, too. If bad weather makes them lose their crop, they will not be hurt as badly as the small farmer. Small farmers have more to lose. They need the money from the year's produce to live and pay bills.

Company farms give jobs to many local people. No special training is needed. An education is not needed to find work. People from other countries can work on farms even if their English is poor.

Small farms once had an important place in America in the past. Now the country has changed. So farming must also change to meet the needs of a growing nation.

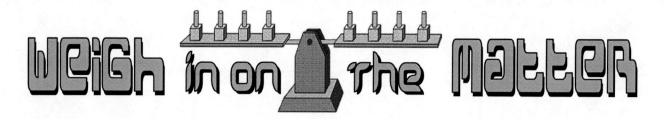

Weigh in on the Matter

Often there is no RIGHT or WRONG answer to a question. There are just different views. You have read the two views about farming. Now tell what you think.

DIRECTIONS: Mark an X to show where you stand on each point. Then tell why you put your X where you did.

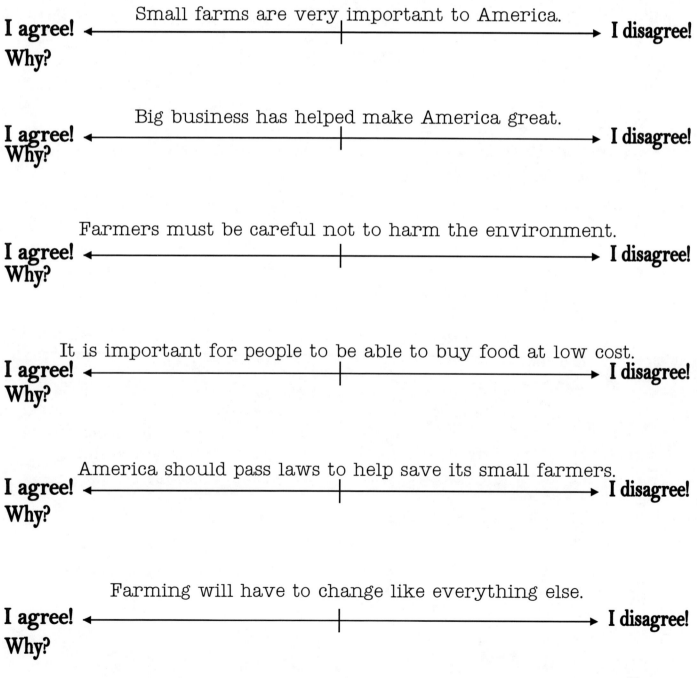

Small farms are very important to America.

I agree! ←————————————————————→ **I disagree!**
Why?

Big business has helped make America great.

I agree! ←————————————————————→ **I disagree!**
Why?

Farmers must be careful not to harm the environment.

I agree! ←————————————————————→ **I disagree!**
Why?

It is important for people to be able to buy food at low cost.

I agree! ←————————————————————→ **I disagree!**
Why?

America should pass laws to help save its small farmers.

I agree! ←————————————————————→ **I disagree!**
Why?

Farming will have to change like everything else.

I agree! ←————————————————————→ **I disagree!**
Why?

Great Lakes!

Springboard:
Students should study the "U.S. Ports Around the Great Lakes" map and answer the questions.

Objective: The student will be able to explain the importance of the Great Lakes to U.S. trade.

Materials: U.S. Ports Around the Great Lakes (Springboard handout)
Fast Facts about the Great Lakes (handout)
A Ship's Captain (handout)
Great (Lakes) Ideas (handout)

Terms to know: **port** - place where ships are loaded and unloaded
peninsula - land with water on three sides
cargo - products and produce carried on a ship, truck, train, etc.
raw materials - natural products used to make other things (wood, iron, etc.)

Procedure:

- After reviewing the Springboard, explain that _in this lesson the student(s) will learn more about the Great Lakes and their importance_.
- Hand out or display "Fast Facts about the Great Lakes." Have the student(s) study the graphs and answer the questions. _(Superior is the largest, longest, and deepest, but has a relatively small population density. Have them compare the data with the Springboard map to help draw conclusions. For example, there are dense populations around Lakes Erie and Michigan, because there are big cities with industries there.)_
- Hand out "A Ship's Captain." Read the narrative together or have the student(s) read it independently. They should then work individually or in groups to complete the "Great (Lakes) Ideas" handout.
- Have them share their ideas and discuss. _(Answers may vary but should highlight key points about the region mentioned in the lesson.)_ During the discussion, point out that _the letters, "HOMES," provide an easy way to remember the names of the Great Lakes._

U.S. Ports Around the Great Lakes

What can you say is true based on the map?
- A. Canada and the United States trade many products.
- B. The Great Lakes are important to American business.
- C. Canada does not have any ports on the Great Lakes.
- D. The U.S. does most of its shipping in the Great Lakes.

The small map at the top shows that the St. Lawrence River
- A. lies inside Canada's borders.
- B. is within the United States.
- C. connects the Great Lakes.
- D. is a route to the Atlantic.

What do you think is **MOST LIKELY** true based on the two maps?
- A. Many products are made near the Great Lakes.
- B. The area around the Great Lakes is very rural.
- C. Great Lakes' ports are used mainly for tourism.
- D. The Great Lakes are not important waterways.

What can you say is true based on the map?
- A. Canada and the United States trade many products.
- B. The Great Lakes are important to American business. *
- C. Canada does not have any ports on the Great Lakes.
- D. The U.S. does most of its shipping in the Great Lakes.

(A and D cannot be determined, and C is false since the title states that the map is of U.S ports.)

The small map at the top shows that the St. Lawrence River
- A. lies inside Canada's borders.
- B. is within the United States.
- C. connects the Great Lakes.
- D. is a route to the Atlantic. *

(The inset map shows the part of the St. Lawrence River that is not shown on the larger map.)

What do you think is **MOST LIKELY** true based on the two maps?
- A. Many products are made near the Great Lakes. *
- B. The area around the Great Lakes is very rural.
- C. Great Lakes' ports are used mainly for tourism.
- D. The Great Lakes are not important waterways.

(B and D are false based on the number of port cities /towns; C is unlikely. A makes sense because products made in the area can be shipped to markets.)

Fast Facts about the Great Lakes

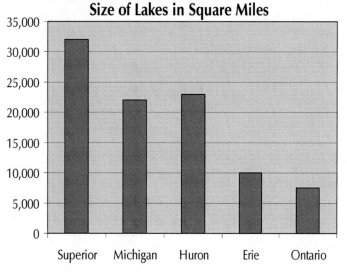

Size of Lakes in Square Miles

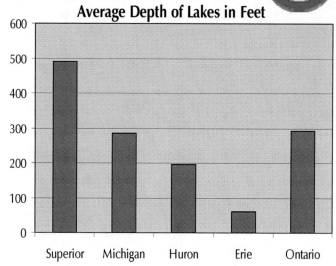

Average Depth of Lakes in Feet

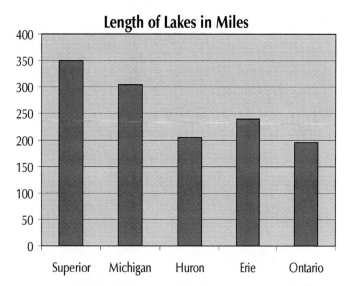

Length of Lakes in Miles

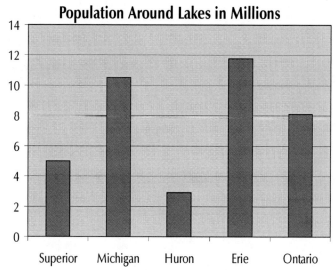

Population Around Lakes in Millions

Which of the Great Lakes is the:

- Largest?

- Smallest?

- Deepest?

- Longest?

- Shortest?

- Most populated?

- Least populated?

- Anything else you can figure out from the graphs?

A Ship's Captain

I've spent my whole life on the Great Lakes. I grew up on the upper peninsula of Michigan. I knew since I was a boy I wanted to work on the water. Now I captain a cargo ship. I can tell you how important these lakes are to the region and the U.S.

Many kinds of cargo are shipped on the Great Lakes. Raw materials, factory goods, farm produce, and fish are all sent away on ships to be sold. The St. Lawrence Seaway, which opened in 1959, lets ships travel to places all over the world. That project dug the St. Lawrence River deeper so big ships could get in and out of the lakes. But it also made the lake water muddy. The same thing happens each time work is done on the Seaway.

There are many raw materials In the Great Lakes region. Wood, coal, iron ore, and more are used in area factories. Some of the raw materials are sold to other places. Both raw materials and factory-made goods are shipped out on the lakes. Steel, cars, and car parts were among the region's biggest products for a long time. Now fewer factory goods are sold as other countries' sales have grown.

Almost 1/3 of all U.S. farm products are from the Great Lakes region. Milk, corn, soybeans, cows, and hogs are the top sellers, but other farm products are also sold. Though there are fewer factories today, they still cause pollution problems. Soil and farm chemicals drain into the water. Pollution kills fish and harms the lakes in other ways. Farms are important but can cause problems for the Great Lakes, too.

Fish have always been an important product of the Great Lakes. Lake trout, whitefish, yellow perch, and other kinds have been taken from the lakes for many years, but their numbers are down now. In the late 1800's, fisherman had record catches of nearly 150 million pounds a year. Now they only get about 20 million pounds.

Water from the lakes is used in making power for the region. It is used for steam that runs power plants. Water is also used to cool the plants' machines. Power plants use a great deal of water. In fact one plant in Wisconsin uses more water than the whole city of Chicago! Of course people need water to live, so the high level of use can be a problem.

Tourists bring money to the Great Lakes region. People come to enjoy the great beauty. They come to hunt, fish, camp, hike, boat, and swim. Keeping the area clean is important for area tourism.

You can see that the Great Lakes are very important. They offer jobs, electric power, shipping, and food. They are also home to many kinds of plants and animals.

Great (Lakes) Ideas

DIRECTIONS: List as many answers as you can for each.

What's So Great about the Great Lakes?

What Can Go Wrong with the Great Lakes?

What Can Be Done to Protect the Great Lakes?

High and Dry

Springboard:
   Students should study "Southwest Cities' Climates" and compare and contrast the cities. *(Both cities have hot summers, cool winters, low levels of rainfall, peak temperatures in July, and similar year-round temperatures. Phoenix is drier and warmer than Dallas. May and September have opposite rainfall patterns, and Dallas, while dry, is not in a desert like Phoenix.)*

Objective: The student will be able to generally describe the climate and some physical features of the Southwest Region.

Materials: Southwest Cities' Climates (Springboard handout)
                      Southwest Features... (handout)

Terms to know: **desert** - area that gets less than ten inches of rainfall per year
                      basin - a low area drained by a river
                      range - large tract of grassy, open land where animals can graze
                      plain - area of level, open land
                      escarpment - long, steep cliff at the edge of a plateau

Procedure:
- During discussion of the Springboard, explain that _the Southwestern United States as a whole is a very dry region. Much of it is desert but even areas like Dallas/Fort Worth that aren't officially deserts are still very dry. Fires are a constant problem in the region_. Go on to explain that _in this lesson the student(s) will learn more about the physical geography of the Southwest_.

- Hand out copies of "Southwest Features..." The student(s) should work individually, in pairs, or small groups to identify types of physical features in the area and use the Internet or other sources find to information about each.
- Have them share their information, pictures, etc. and discuss. *(Answers will vary. The definitions above offer some features. Others include mountains, plateaus, rivers, coastal flats, rivers, etc.)*
- The student(s) should then create a poster or booklet about one of the features they examine.

Southwest Cities' Climates

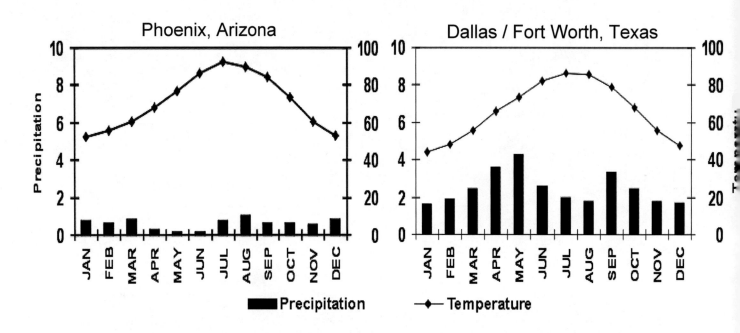

Five ways the climate of Phoenix, Arizona is LIKE the climate of Dallas, Texas are:

1. _____

2. _____

3. _____

4. _____

5. _____

Five ways the climate of Phoenix, Arizona is UNLIKE the climate of Dallas, Texas are:

1. _____

2. _____

3. _____

4. _____

5. _____

SOUTHWEST FEATURES...

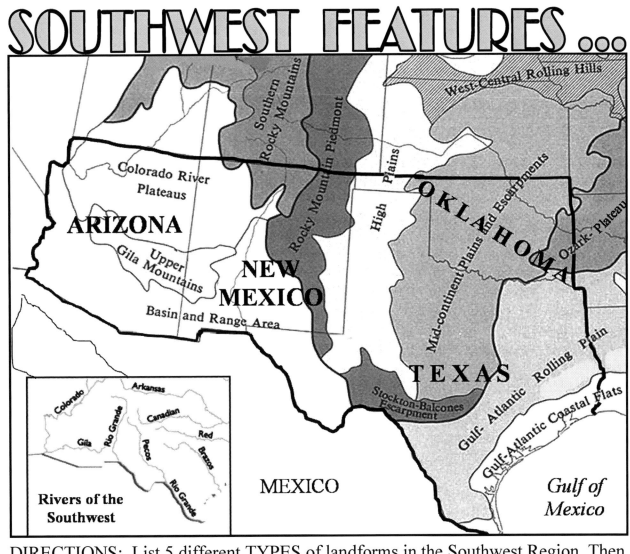

DIRECTIONS: List 5 different TYPES of landforms in the Southwest Region. Then find information or pictures and take notes about each one.

1. _____

_____

2. _____

_____

_____

3. _____

_____

_____

4. _____

_____

_____

5. _____

_____

_____

Growing by Leaps and Bounds

Springboard:
Students should study "Population Growth"
and answer the questions.

Objective: The student will be able to explain the rapid rate of growth in the Southwest and the problems it is causing, particularly in regards to water.

Materials:
Population Growth (Springboard handout)
Census and the Cities (handout)
Water Planning Board Project Requests (handout)
Committee Report (handout)

Terms to know:
suburb - area outside a city where people live
environmental group - people working to protect the earth and nature
dam - a structure built in a waterway to control the flow of water, often forming a lake behind it

Procedure:

- After reviewing the Springboard, explain that *this lesson further examines how population growth is affecting the Southwest Region*.
- Distribute the "Census and the Cities" handout and have the student(s) answer the questions.
- Have them share their answers and discuss. *(Suggested answers:*
  1. *Five of the ten fastest growing cities were in the Southwest.*
  2. *Yuma, AZ, McAllen/Mission, TX, Austin, TX, Phoenix/Mesa, AZ, and Laredo, TX.)*
  3. *Answers may vary and include good climate, job opportunities, etc.*
  4. *Problems include those normally associated with growth: pollution, traffic, overcrowded schools, etc., but in the Southwest a major concern is WATER, since the region is so dry.*
- Explain that *in this lesson the student(s) will serve on a "committee" of the Water Planning Board of a large city in the desert Southwest to consider the water issue and report their recommendations*.
- Distribute the "Water Planning Board Project Requests" and "Committee Report" handouts. Tell the student(s) that *this month's meeting of the Water Planning Board is now called to order*. **For group instruction** divide students into groups to review the project requests and make recommendations on the "Committee Report" form. **For individualized instruction** work with your student as a "committee" of two.
- Have the student(s) share their ideas and discuss. *(Answers may vary, but students should be able to support their ideas with logical reasons.)*

POPULATION GROWTH

Top 15 States by Percent of Population Growth, 1990-2000

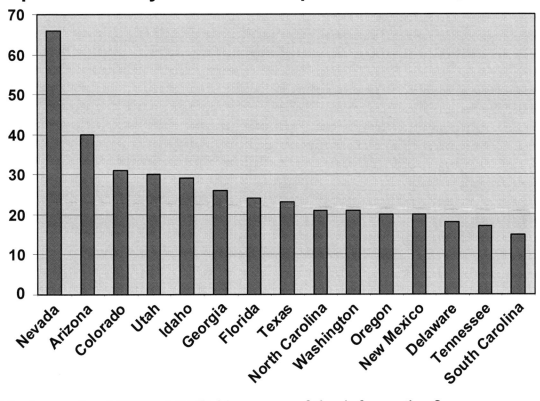

What was the **MOST LIKELY** source of the information?
- A. Congress
- B. U.S. banks
- C. state taxes
- D. census data

Arizona grew at a rate of about
- A. 40 people.
- B. 400 people.
- C. 40 percent.
- D. 400 percent.

What other states from the Southwest region ranked in the top 15?
- A. Colorado and Delaware
- B. Texas and New Mexico
- C. Nevada and South Carolina
- D. Washington and Tennessee

Which of these population problems would be **WORSE** for the Southwest than some other regions?
- A. traffic jams
- B. air pollution
- C. crowded schools
- D. not enough water

Top 15 States by Percent of Population Growth, 1990-2000

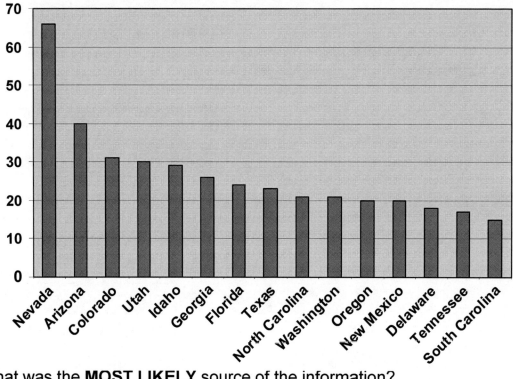

What was the **MOST LIKELY** source of the information?

A. Congress   C. state taxes

B. U.S. banks   D. census data *

(Students should recognize that census information is used for a variety of purposes.)

Arizona grew at a rate of about

A. 40 people.   C. 40 percent. *

B. 400 people.   D. 400 percent.

(Make sure students understand the meaning of this percentage. Arizona's population grew by 40 people for every hundred in the state in 1990.)

What other states from the Southwest region ranked in the top 15?

A. Colorado and Delaware   *(By this point in studying*

B. Texas and New Mexico *   *U.S. geography, students*

C. Nevada and South Carolina   *should be able to eliminate*

D. Washington and Tennessee   *the incorrect choices.)*

Which of these population problems would be **WORSE** for the Southwest than some other regions?

A. traffic jams   C. crowded schools

B. air pollution   D. not enough water *

(Choices A-C are typical problems related to population growth. D would only apply to places with dry climates like the Southwest.)

CENSUS AND THE CITIES

Top 10 Metropolitan Areas in the U.S.
Ranked by Growth from 2000 Census

Rank	City, State	% Growth
1.	Las Vegas, Nevada	83%
2.	Naples, Florida	65%
3.	Yuma, Arizona	50%
4.	McAllen / Mission, Texas	49%
5.	Austin, Texas	48%
6.	Fayetteville, Arkansas	48%
7.	Boise City, Idaho	46%
8.	Phoenix / Mesa, Arizona	45%
9.	Laredo, Texas	45%
10.	Provo, Utah	40%

1. How many of the top 10 ranked cities are in the Southwest Region?

2. Which cities are they?

3. Why do you think these cities have grown at such a fast rate?

4. Given what you know about the Southwest, what are some problems you think this growth could cause?

WATER PLANNING BOARD

PROJECT REQUESTS

1. A builder wants to build a new lake community in the suburbs of your city. There are 200 homes planned along with a lake for boating, skiing, and swimming. The homes will cost a lot so the city can make money from taxes on them.

   The builder has built other neighborhoods in the area. All have been very nice places to live. Many people like this builder and the lifestyle of the communities.

2. A foreign auto maker wants to build a factory just outside the city. The plant will bring many new jobs to the area and tax dollars as well. It will also bring many new people.

   As in most urban areas, jobs are always needed. Still, you must think about the large amount of water and power the factory will need to run. You must also think about the homes needed to house the people moving to the city.

3. The schools in the area are very crowded. The school district wants to build a new elementary school. They want the school to be close to the children who will go there. The problem is the only land left is partly a wetland. This means that some of the wetland will need to be filled in.

   The children's parents like the school district's choice of a site. The students would be able to walk or take a short bus ride to get there. Some environmental groups do not like the choice. They don't want any of the wetland to be filled in.

4. The state wants to build a new dam. It would be on a nearby river that supplies the city's water. The dam will be used to make electricity for the city. It will also form a lake which will attract visitors and their tourist dollars. However, the river below the dam would be smaller. There would be less water for the city to draw from. The state has asked the city for its views on the dam.

COMMITTEE REPORT

Project # 1.

How would this project help the city?	How would this project hurt the city?

Should this project be built?

Project # 2.

How would this project help the city?	How would this project hurt the city?

Should this project be built?

Project # 3.

How would this project help the city?	How would this project hurt the city?

Should this project be built?

Project # 4.

How would this project help the city?	How would this project hurt the city?

Should this project be built?

El Rio

Springboard:
Students should study the "On the Border" map and information and answer the questions.

Objective: The student will be able to explain the issues surrounding the U.S. and Mexico border.

Materials:
On the Border (Springboard handout)
Look at It This Way (handout)
Look at the View! (handout)

Terms to know:
illegal - against the law
immigration - movement into a country to live or work

Procedure:
- Review the Springboard questions and answers. During discussion of the last question, have the student(s) suggest the types of problems that could be caused by people moving across the border easily. *(Answers will vary, but could include illegal immigrants and terrorists coming across, along with drugs, weapons, or other dangerous items.)* Go on to explain that *in this lesson students will learn more about the U.S.-Mexican border*.
- Hand out or display "Look at It This Way." Read the four viewpoints together or have the student(s) read them and discuss the pros and cons of Mexican immigration.
- Then hand out "Look at the View!" Explain that *this drawing is called an editorial cartoon. Newspapers and writers give their opinions of people and events in writing or in pictures. Editorial cartoons are meant to make a point and make people think about problems*.
- Have the student(s) study the cartoon and answer the questions. Then have them share their answers and discuss.
- **EXTENSION:** Have the student(s) watch the news or talk to their parents to find out more about the immigration issue. The student(s) could conduct interviews of school and community leaders to learn how their community is affected by immigration.

ON THE BORDER

The border between the U.S. and Mexico is 2,000 miles long. It spans four American and six Mexican states. The Rio Grande River forms the border between Texas and four of the Mexican states.

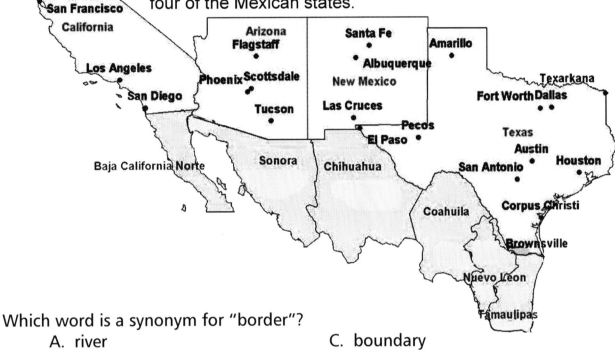

Which word is a synonym for "border"?
- A. river
- B. state
- C. boundary
- D. country

What four U.S. states border Mexico?
- A. Baja California, Sonora, Chihuahua, and Coahuila
- B. San Diego, Tucson, Las Cruces, and Brownsville
- C. Los Angeles, Phoenix, El Paso, and Corpus Christi
- D. California, Arizona, New Mexico, and Texas

The Rio Grande River is between
- A. Nuevo Leon and Tamaulipas.
- B. San Antonio and Coahuila.
- C. Tucson and Sonora.
- D. Pecos and El Paso.

What problem do you think the border could cause?
- A. Many people would be poor.
- B. Americans would travel to Mexico.
- C. Mexico and the U.S. would be friends.
- D. People could cross the border too easily.

The border between the U.S. and Mexico is 2,000 miles long. It spans four American and six Mexican states. The Rio Grande River forms the border between Texas and four of the Mexican states.

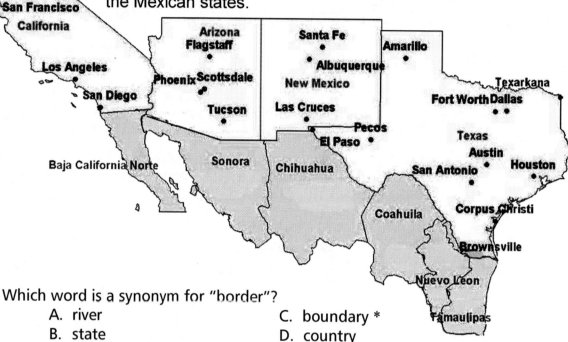

Which word is a synonym for "border"?
  A. river
  B. state
  C. boundary *
  D. country
(Even students who don't know what a boundary is should be able to figure this out by process of elimination.)

What four U.S. states border Mexico?
  A. Baja California, Sonora, Chihuahua, and Coahuila
  B. San Diego, Tucson, Las Cruces, and Brownsville
  C. Los Angeles, Phoenix, El Paso, and Corpus Christi
  D. California, Arizona, New Mexico, and Texas *
(The city names are in black type, and the state names are in grey. Students should know that the U.S. is north of Mexico and recognize the state names.)

The Rio Grande River is between
  A. Nuevo Leon and Tamaulipas.
  B. San Antonio and Coahuila. *
  C. Tucson and Sonora.
  D. Pecos and El Paso.

(The paragraph says the river separates Texas and Mexico. The only places on either side of that border are in Choice B.)

What problem do you think the border could cause?
  A. Many people would be poor.
  B. Americans would travel to Mexico.
  C. Mexico and the U.S. would be friends.
  D. People could cross the border too easily. *
(Choices B and C are not problems, and Choice A would not be CAUSED by the border. D is a logical answer.)

LOOK AT IT THIS WAY

The United States is too crowded now. Many Americans have trouble finding jobs. It is not a good idea to let people cross the border from Mexico to come here.

It is illegal to cross the border without the right papers. There are ways for immigrants to come to the U.S. Many do come legally. We just can't have illegal immigrants come in. They take Americans' jobs.

Illegal immigrants also cost the U.S. money. The country has to pay to send their children to school. It must pay for their health care. There are many costs. This is why we must stop people from crossing into the United States from Mexico!

The United States is a nation of immigrants. Native Americans are the only true natives. Every other American's family came from some other country.

Americans enjoy the best of everything. We eat foods and drive cars from all over the world. Our clothes are made in other lands. We just can't shut America off from other people or countries.

People come to America for jobs and better lives. Immigrants come from Mexico for the same reasons. These people help the U.S. They do jobs that are hard to fill. They spend money in U.S. stores. We should welcome them here!

IMMIGRATION

Farmers, builders, and other business owners know that the U.S. needs workers from Mexico. Immigrants cross the border for work and better lives. The work they do is hard. They take jobs that few Americans want.

Mexican workers are good at their jobs. They work hard and help the country. Immigrant workers help keep the cost of U.S. goods such as farm produce low.

If we force an end to Mexican immigration, people will hide. They will not want to send their children to school. They will not go to doctors. That would be too cruel to do to good, hardworking people!

It is wrong to let Mexican immigrants come to the United States for work. These people are poor in Mexico. When they come to America, they take any job they can find. They work too much for too little pay.

More and more companies want these illegal workers because they can pay them less than they would pay Americans. Illegals take American jobs and keep pay low.

Illegal immigration also puts us all in danger. If Mexican workers can come into the U.S., so can drug dealers and others who can do us harm. We must do all we can stop illegal immigration!

69

Look at the View!

1. What is the cartoon about? _____
_____

2. Who is the person in the cartoon? _____
_____

3. What symbols are in the cartoon? What do they mean? _____
_____
_____
_____

4. Explain what you think the artist was trying to say? _____
_____
_____
_____
_____
_____
_____
_____

Rocky Roads

Springboard:

Students should read "Trails West" and answer the questions.

(1. The Bozeman, Oregon, California, Mormon, and Santa Fe Trails all started in Illinois or Missouri and ended in various western states. 2. Colorado, California, Idaho, Montana, Nevada, Oregon, Utah, Washington, and Wyoming.
3. People moved west for free or inexpensive farmland, to mine for gold, for religious freedom, to work on the transcontinental railroad, to ranch, etc.)

Objective: The student will be able to generally describe the land and climate of the western region.

Materials: Trails West (Springboard handout)
Moving In for a Closer Look (handout)

Terms to know: **continent** - one of seven great land masses on the earth (North America, South America, Europe, Asia, Africa, Australia, and Antarctica)
rain shadow - area with little rainfall due to a mountain range

Procedure:
- After reviewing the Springboard, explain that *in this lesson the student(s) will learn more about the geography of the West.*
- Distribute "Moving In for a Closer Look." Read the handout together, and discuss, making sure the student(s) understand the rain shadow effect. Explain that *as moist air from the ocean moves inland, it rises and is cooled, dropping most of its moisture in the form of rain or snow on the western side of the mountain range. Most of the land inland on the eastern side of the mountain ranges is much drier. The resulting deserts or grasslands in what is called the "Empty Interior" are used for grazing cattle.*
- Review the directions and have the student(s) work individually to write their own "sources" about fictitious trips west, using factual details from the lesson.
- **EXTENSION:** The student(s) could write short stories about traveling to the West as a language arts/social studies cross-over activity.
- Have students share their accounts and discuss.

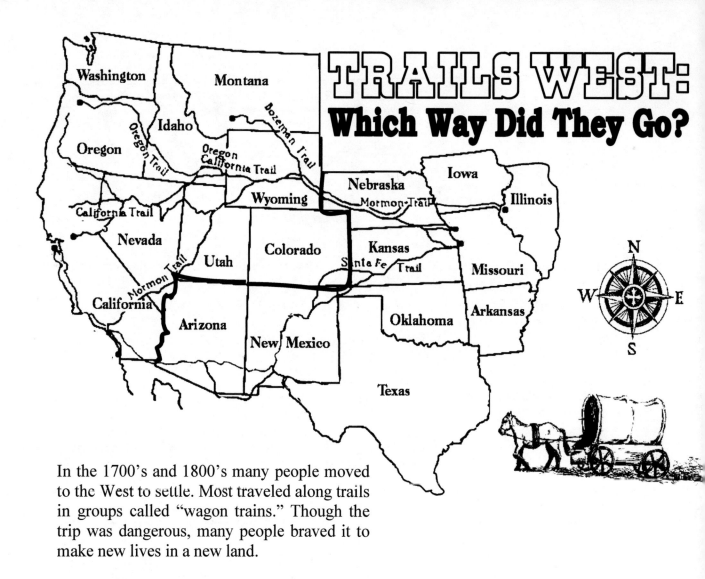

TRAILS WEST:
Which Way Did They Go?

In the 1700's and 1800's many people moved to the West to settle. Most traveled along trails in groups called "wagon trains." Though the trip was dangerous, many people braved it to make new lives in a new land.

1. Find 3 trails on the map. Where do they begin and end?

2. Which states on the map are in "The West"?

3. What are some reasons why people might have wanted to brave a dangerous trip to move West?

MOVING IN FOR A CLOSER LOOK

The Cascade and Sierra Nevada Mountain Ranges line the U.S. Pacific coast at or near the coastline. Beyond the mountains lies The Empty Interior. This area is mostly dry. Rains that move inland from the ocean are blocked by the mountains' rain shadow. Heavy rains fall on the west side of the mountains. Far less rain falls on their eastern side.

Further inland are the Rocky Mountains. This huge mountain range, like others, has many streams that run down its sides. These streams form larger rivers such as the Colorado as they flow downward to the sea.

DIRECTIONS: Pretend you are a settler going west across the mountains and The Empty Interior. Write a paragraph or two about your journey. Tell what you see, hear, and do. Be creative! _____

_____

_____

_____

_____

_____

_____

_____

_____

_____

_____

_____

_____

_____

_____

_____

Shake, Rattle, and Roll

Objective: The student will be able to explain the frequency of earthquakes in the West due to its location in the Ring of Fire.

Materials:
Ring of Fire (Springboard handout)
Map or globe with map key
Livin' in the Ring of Fire (handout)
Where Are the Earthquakes? (handout)

Terms to know:
earthquake - a shaking of the earth
volcano - an opening in the earth that spews out lava, ash, and gases
tsunami - a very large ocean wave caused by an earthquake or volcano in the ocean
map key - part of a map that tells what the colors and shapes on the map mean

Procedure:

- After discussing the Springboard, explain that *in this lesson the student(s) will learn more about earthquakes and volcanoes.*

- Hand out "Livin' in the Ring of Fire" and have them point out a few things they notice about the information *(volcanoes are in the West, Alaska has the most earthquakes, etc.)*. If the student(s) fail to mention it, point out the map key, and have them explain why maps include keys and review the definition.

- After a brief discussion, *explain that the student(s) will be using the earthquake information to color or shade in the "Where Are the Earthquakes?" map.* Have the student(s) suggest how to create the map keys and explain what the colors or shading could look like *(colored-in boxes, circles, etc. labeled as to what they mean)*.

- The student(s) should work individually or in pairs to fill in the map, including a map key that explains colors or shading. They should also answer the question at the bottom of the page.

- Have the student(s) share their maps and ideas. *(Answers may vary, but should reflect the fact that the West has more earthquake activity because it is located in the Ring of Fire.)*

- **EXTENSION:** There are a number of earthquake-related activities and real-time pictures showing where earthquakes are occurring that the student(s) might enjoy on the U.S. Geological Survey (USGS) website @ **http://earthquake.usgs.gov/learning/kids.php**.

RING OF FIRE

The Ring of Fire is a zone of many earthquakes and volcanoes. 90% of the world's earthquakes and 75% of volcanoes are in the zone. Both can cause great damage and loss of life. Earthquakes and volcanoes in the ocean can also trigger tsunamis. Tsunamis are huge waves that hit shorelines. They can be terrible!

Unlike storms, scientists can not be sure when earthquakes, volcanoes, and tsunamis will hit. People living in the Ring of Fire know that they and their homes are always at some risk. Still, many years can pass with no problems at all.

Many millions of people live in the Ring of Fire. How do you think living ther might effect their lives? _____

_____

_____

_____

_____

What special things, if any, do you think they might have to do? _____

_____

_____

_____

_____

LIVIN' IN THE RING OF FIRE

DIRECTIONS: Use the earthquake information to shade or color the "Where Are the Earthquakes?" U.S. map. Compare your map with the map of "America's Volcanoes."

Earthquakes in the United States in the 30 years from 1974-2003

States	# of earthquakes	States	# of earthquakes	States	# of earthquakes
Alaska	12,053	Illinois	17	Massachusetts	2
California	4,895	Oklahoma	17	Michigan	2
Hawaii	1533	Maine	16	Minnesota	2
Nevada	778	New York	16	Mississippi	2
Washington	424	Alabama	15	New Jersey	2
Idaho	404	Kentucky	15	Louisiana	1
Wyoming	217	South Carolina	10	Rhode Island	1
Montana	186	South Dakota	10	West Virginia	1
Utah	139	Virginia	10	Connecticut	0
Oregon	73	Nebraska	8	Delaware	0
New Mexico	38	Ohio	8	Florida	0
Arkansas	34	Georgia	7	Iowa	0
Arizona	32	Indiana	6	Maryland	0
Colorado	24	New Hampshire	6	North Dakota	0
Tennessee	22	Pennsylvania	6	Vermont	0
Missouri	21	Kansas	4	Wisconsin	0
Texas	20	North Carolina	3	TOTAL	21,080

America's Volcanoes

Most are not active, but 18 are said to be at a "high risk" of erupting:
2 in Hawaii; 5 in Alaska; 4 in Washington; 4 in Oregon; and 2 in California.

Map Key
⚲ Volcano

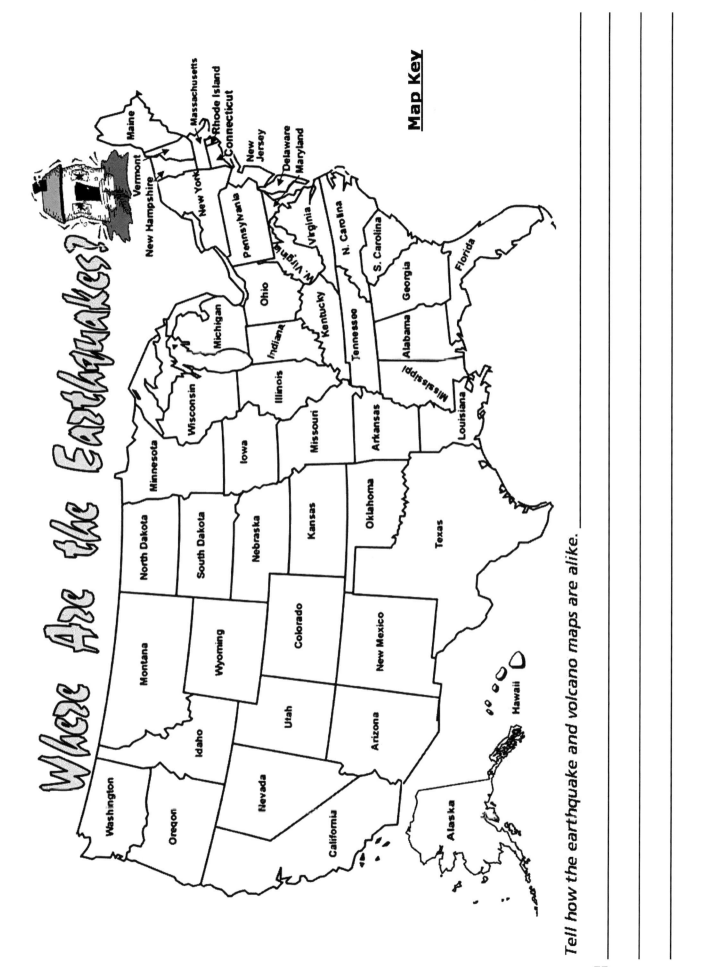

Where Are the Earthquakes?

Map Key

Tell how the earthquake and volcano maps are alike.

Paradise Found

Objective: The student will be able to describe the physical geography and culture of Hawaii.

Materials: IsLand Land (Springboard handout)
Island Girl (handout)
WWW.Hawaii Web - (handout)

Terms to know: **map scale** - part of a map that explains the true size of land, water, etc. (ex. 1 inch = 200 miles)
culture - way of life
conservation - careful use of resources to make sure they last
language - system of speaking / writing used in a country or by a group of people (English, Spanish, etc.)
capital - city that is the seat (place) of government

Procedure:

- During discussion of the last Springboard question, have the student(s) identify the islands, Honolulu as the state's capital, Hilo as the largest city on the island of Hawaii, and Kilauea as an active volcano. Point out that *the islands were formed by volcanoes, but most no longer erupt*. Then go on to explain that *in this lesson the student(s) will learn more about the island state of Hawaii and its "culture"* (review the term).
- Hand out "Island Girl" and "WWW.Hawaii Web." Read the handout together or have the student(s) read the narrative and use it along with other other sources to create a Hawaii Web.
- Have the student(s) work individually, in pairs, small groups using the handout to fill in information about each topic. A good information source to information about island activities is **www.hawaiiweb.com**.
- Have the student(s) share their web information and discuss.

Island Land

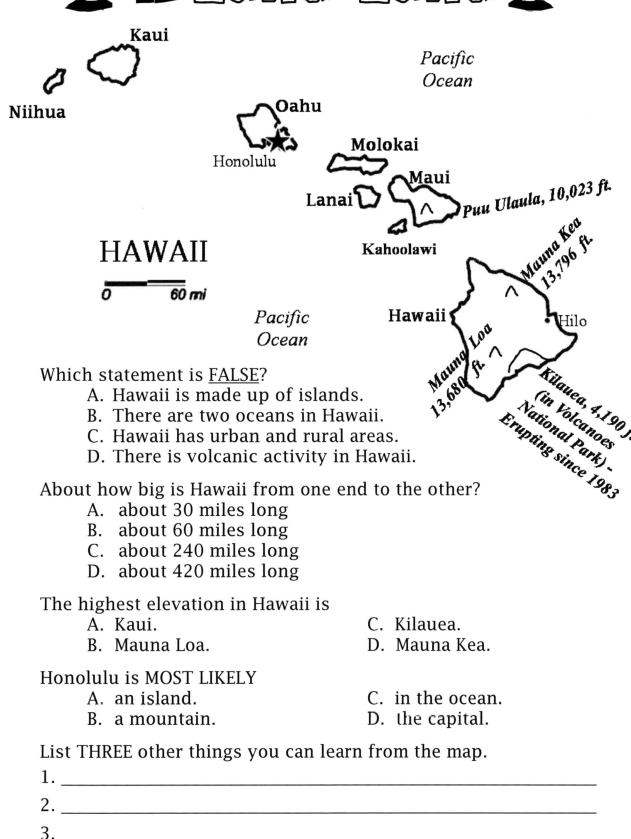

Kaui

Niihua

Pacific Ocean

Oahu

Honolulu

Molokai

Maui

Lanai

Kahoolawi

Puu Ulaula, 10,023 ft.

HAWAII

0   60 mi

Pacific Ocean

Hawaii

Hilo

Mauna Kea 13,796 ft.

Mauna Loa 13,680 ft.

Kilauea, 4,190 ft. (in Volcanoes National Park) - Erupting since 1983

Which statement is <u>FALSE</u>?
A. Hawaii is made up of islands.
B. There are two oceans in Hawaii.
C. Hawaii has urban and rural areas.
D. There is volcanic activity in Hawaii.

About how big is Hawaii from one end to the other?
A. about 30 miles long
B. about 60 miles long
C. about 240 miles long
D. about 420 miles long

The highest elevation in Hawaii is
A. Kaui.
B. Mauna Loa.
C. Kilauea.
D. Mauna Kea.

Honolulu is MOST LIKELY
A. an island.
B. a mountain.
C. in the ocean.
D. the capital.

List THREE other things you can learn from the map.

1. _____

2. _____

3. _____

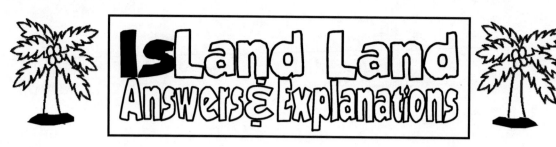

Island Land
Answers & Explanations

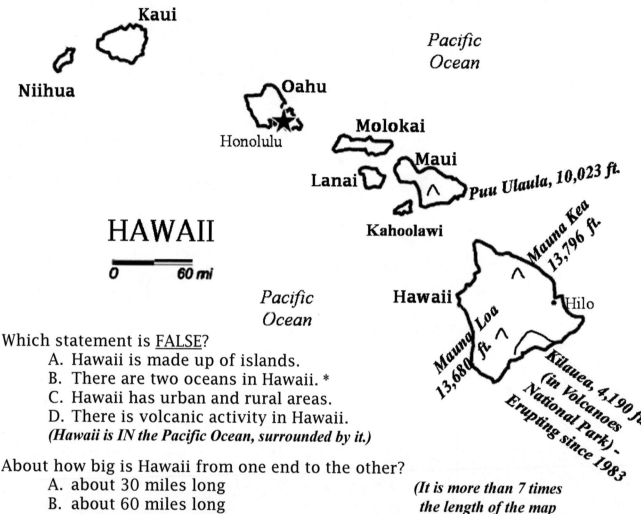

Which statement is <u>FALSE</u>?
    A. Hawaii is made up of islands.
    B. There are two oceans in Hawaii. *
    C. Hawaii has urban and rural areas.
    D. There is volcanic activity in Hawaii.
(Hawaii is IN the Pacific Ocean, surrounded by it.)

About how big is Hawaii from one end to the other?
    A. about 30 miles long
    B. about 60 miles long
    C. about 240 miles long
    D. about 420 miles long *

(It is more than 7 times the length of the map scale, so it is more than 420 miles long.)

The highest elevation in Hawaii is
    A. Kaui.   C. Kilauea.
    B. Mauna Loa.   D. Mauna Kea. *

(Mauna Kea is higher than the 2nd highest mountain, Mauna Loa.)

Honolulu is MOST LIKELY
    A. an island.   C. in the ocean.
    B. a mountain.   D. the capital. *

(Students will likely know that stars on a map indicate the capital city.)

List THREE other things you can learn from the map.
Answers will vary and could include: Hawaii is an archipelago or a chain of islands; there are 5 main islands; Hawaii is the largest and Kahoolawi is the smallest island; Kiauea is an active volcano; Honolulu is a major city located on the island of Oahu; Hilo is another important city located on the island of Hawaii; etc.

Island Girl

Aloha, I am Lani. I live on the island of Hawaii, the largest of our state. Unlike most of the people here today, I am a native Hawaiian. My family lived in the islands long before the many immigrants came from China, Japan, America and other places. Hawaiians are proud to be part of the great state of Hawaii. Yet we are also very proud of our native culture.

We love our islands and the sea. We believe we are "children of the land." From the old times the land has given us all we need: food, clothes, houses, tools, canoes, everything. We take from the land and care for it in return. Conservation is most important to us. If we harm the land or water, we harm ourselves.

Hawaiian people are very kind to others. We welcome visitors and new people. Hawaiians love to share what we have with others. We want people to enjoy the great beauty of our land. Our kind ways are called the "aloha spirit."

When people come to visit Hawaii, we like to give them leis *(lays)*. Leis are strings of flowers to wear around the neck. Another way we welcome visitors is with our native dance, the hula. Every move in the hula means something to us. The hula and the songs that go with it tell stories of Hawaiian gods and heroes. In the old days the hula was danced as part of our religion. Today we dance it for our joy and to make others happy. Many young women like me go to schools to learn to dance.

People who come to Hawaii today find that people here speak English. This is because many white people came to grow sugar cane and pineapples. They taught English to the Hawaiians. We have our own language, but not many people speak it well now. My family sometimes speaks Hawaiian at home so we can learn it, but we all speak English, too.

Another way Hawaiians are different from other people here is our food. Like others we eat much fish and seafood because we live in the islands. We also eat fruits like bananas, strawberries, and coconuts. Our most important food, though, is poi *(poy)*. It is a Hawaiian food made from the root of the taro plant. The taro root is pounded into a purple paste that we eat with our fingers. I love poi, but I know others may not like it. Another food we eat a lot of is Spam, a kind of canned ham. It is fairly new to Hawaii, but we have found many good ways to cook it.

I hope that one day you will come to visit Hawaii, if you have never been here. You can see for yourself how lovely it is and how kind my people are.

WWW.Hawaii Web

DIRECTIONS: Use information from the lesson and other sources as needed to fill in this Hawaii Web.

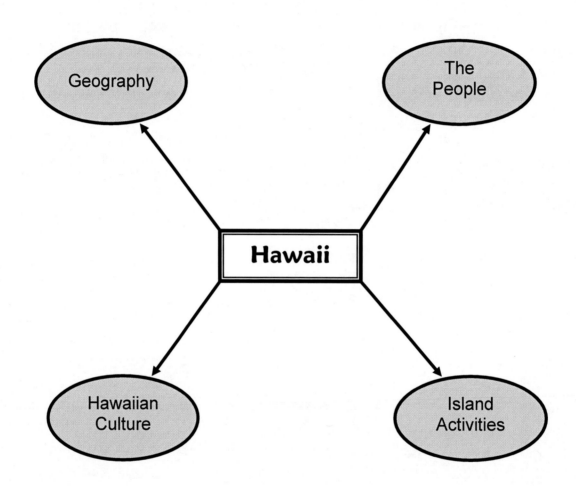

Geography

The People

Hawaii

Hawaiian Culture

Island Activities

WWW Hawaii Web
Suggestions for Answers

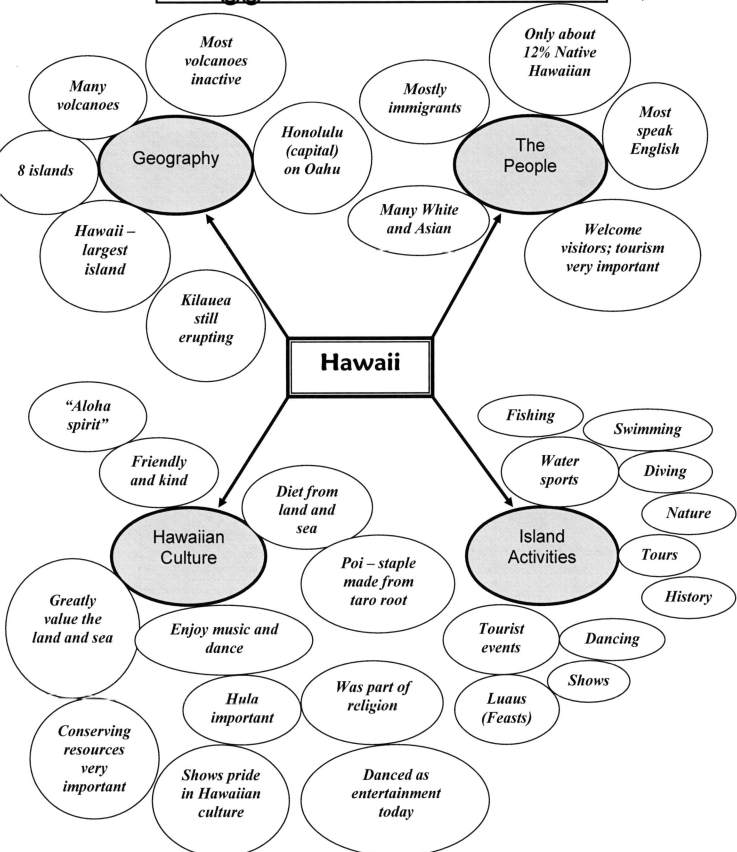

Geography

Most volcanoes inactive

Many volcanoes

8 islands

Honolulu (capital) on Oahu

Hawaii – largest island

Kilauea still erupting

The People

Only about 12% Native Hawaiian

Mostly immigrants

Most speak English

Many White and Asian

Welcome visitors; tourism very important

Hawaii

Hawaiian Culture

"Aloha spirit"

Friendly and kind

Diet from land and sea

Poi – staple made from taro root

Greatly value the land and sea

Enjoy music and dance

Was part of religion

Hula important

Conserving resources very important

Shows pride in Hawaiian culture

Danced as entertainment today

Island Activities

Fishing

Swimming

Water sports

Diving

Nature

Tours

History

Tourist events

Dancing

Shows

Luaus (Feasts)

The Cold, Hard Facts

Springboard
Students should read "About Alaska" and answer the questions.
(The ANWR is in the northeast corner and has ice, mountains, polar bears, seals, elk, flowers and grasses during part of the year, water, fish, some people, etc. It is important to the Arctic region as a home to many endangered animals.)

Objective: The student will be able to explain the controversy over drilling for oil in the Alaskan National Wildlife Refuge (ANWR).

Materials: About Alaska (Springboard handout)
What SHOULD We Do?! (handout)

Terms to know: **refuge** - a place set aside to protect animals, birds, trees, etc.

Procedure:
- During discussion of the Springboard, explain that _besides being home to many animals and some people, the ANWR, like much of Alaska, contains a large amount of oil_. Go on to explain that _oil companies already drill for oil in other parts of the state, but they want to drill in the ANWR to get the oil from there as well_.
- Tell the student(s) that _today's lesson is a group "brainstorming" activity with no right or wrong answers_. Go on to explain that _the goal of brainstorming is to list as many ideas as possible FOR and AGAINST drilling for oil in the Alaskan National Wildlife Refuge_.
- **For group instruction** have the student(s) work in groups to list ideas on their "What SHOULD We Do?!" handout. As they discuss the topic, walk around, encouraging good ideas and making suggestions as needed to stimulate thought. (For example, students will probably know that America needs oil to run its cars and industries, but they may not think about the fact that some countries we get our oil from have problems with terrorism. On the other hand, they will know that animals need a safe place to live, but they may not consider the risk of oil spills.) **For individualized instruction** work with your student to brainstorm ideas, then discuss what he or she thinks is the best course of action. Then, skip to the final step of the Procedures.
- **For group instruction**, ask students what they think is the BEST course of action. Have those who favor drilling stand/sit on one side of the room and those against drilling on the other.
- Lead a debate allowing one student from each side to make a point, the other side respond, and the first team add additional comments. Then allow the second team to introduce a point and two comments. (In large classes it may be a good idea to have students raise their hands to speak, since debates can turn into shouting matches.)
- The student(s) should answer the Objective question about Alaska's oil to summarize what they have learned in this lesson.

ABOUT ALASKA

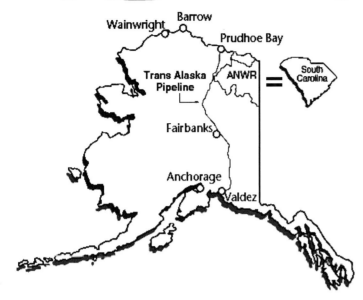

Alaska is the largest state in the U.S. It is about twice as big as Texas, which ranks 2nd. The state has some cities and towns, such as Juneau *(Joo' nō)*, Fairbanks, Barrow, and others. Anchorage is the largest city with about ¼ of a million people.

Places outside of cities and towns have few people at all. The state has 39 mountain ranges, a huge plateau, and a vast coastal plain. Most places in Alaska have more animals than people.

The northern coastal plain is one such place. It is home to the Alaskan National Wildlife Refuge (ANWR). The ANWR is only a small part of the state. Yet even it is as big as South Carolina.

Where in Alaska is the ANWR? _____

_____

_____

What do you think you would see in the ANWR?

_____

_____

_____

_____

Why do you think the ANWR is important to Alaska, the nation, and the world? _____

_____

_____

_____

WHAT SHOULD WE DO?!

DRILL in the ANWR	DON'T DRILL in the ANWR

NOW, write a paragraph to explain what YOU think about this. State your view and give as many reasons as you can to support it.

_____

_____

_____

_____

_____

_____

_____

_____

_____

_____

_____

Hurray for Hollywood!

Springboard:
    Students should read "_____" and answer the questions.
                    (Answers will vary.)

Objective: The student will be able identify some important states, cities, and other important physical and cultural features of the United States.

Materials: _____ (Springboard handout)
                    Symbol Says… (handout)

Terms to know: **symbol** - something that stands for a place, idea, etc.

Procedure:

· After discussing the Springboard and allowing the student(s) to share the symbol(s), explain that *in this lesson the student(s) are going to find or create symbols for places all across the United States as a final look at U.S. geography*.

· Hand out copies of "Symbol Says…" The student(s) should work individually or in pairs using the Internet or other resources to find or make up symbols for a variety of places in the country. They can use existing symbols like flags or other state symbols or make up ones to represent their places. For example, the Rocky Mountains could be represented by ⌇⌃⌃⌃. Encourage the student(s) to be creative, but not silly in their depictions. The purpose of this activity is to help them remember some of the important geographic and cultural features of the country.

· Have the student(s) share their places and symbols, allowing others to try to explain them. They can then explain their reasoning, as appropriate.

· Then have them make cards either by cutting up their handout, or **for group instruction** have them work in pairs or small groups to combine their cards to play "Concentration," matching the places with the symbols that represent them. **For individualized instruction** have the student create additional symbols to play the game.

It sits up high in the Hollywood Hills of Los Angeles, California. It is a symbol of the town. It is also a symbol of the dream we call "Hollywood." That symbol is the Hollywood sign.

The fifty-foot tall letters lit up by 4,000 light bulbs were first put up in 1923. At that time the sign read "Hollywoodland" as an ad for a new home building project. Soon, though, people began coming to Hollywoodland just to see the huge sign.

By the time the sign went up, Hollywood had made a name for itself in films. Four million Americans went to the movies each week! Big movie companies put out silent films with big movie stars.

Charley Chaplin, Buster Keaton, Laurel and Hardy, and Rudolph Valentino were superstars of their day. Mary Pickford, Clara Bow, and other Hollywood women were well-known for their talent and beauty. Young people came to Hollywood to find their dreams. Most never became stars, but a few did.

The sign was for many the symbol of why they came to Hollywood. This is why years later, when the sign was falling down, the city took down the last four letters and fixed the rest. Today it still stands as a symbol of movies and the dreams to be a star.

Which of these titles do you think would be **BEST** for the reading?
    A. "Symbol of a Dream"
    B. "The Hollywood Sign"
    C. "Hollywoodland Stars"
    D. "In the Hollywood Hills"

Explain why you think this is a good title. _____

_____

_____

_____

_____

Draw a symbol for the city or town you live in below. Then explain your symbol.

Symbol Says...

DIRECTIONS: Find or make up symbols for cities, physical features, or other places across the United States. Be sure to include places from all the regions.

Place	Symbol	Place	Symbol

REVIEWING TERMS

PUZZLE CLUES

ACROSS

1 farm products
3 low area drained by a river
5 long, narrow island along a coast
7 area with common features
8 something that makes a place unfit for living things
10 how deep water is
13 level, open land
14 people working to protect the land and nature
16 land with less than ten inches of rain yearly
18 structure built across a river to control water
22 land with water on three sides
24 rolling land near a mountain range
29 opening in the earth that spews lava, etc.
30 land next to an ocean
31 farming
35 having to do with the countryside
37 area with mixed fresh and salt water
39 products carried on a ship
40 writings from a time period
43 one of seven great land masses on the earth
44 land with water all around it
45 high, flat land
48 part of a map that explains colors and symbols
50 long, steep cliff
53 grassland
54 a natural feature
55 are with little rainfall due to mountains
56 against the law
57 system of speaking or writing

DOWN

1 number of people
2 huge wave caused by an earthquake
3 line dividing two countries or states
4 underwater sloping land near shore
6 triangle of land at a river's mouth
9 way something is generally going
11 place where ships load and unload
12 careful use of resources
15 wet, coastal land with streams that rise with the tides
17 place set aside to protect nature
19 large area of open, grazing land
20 shaking of the earth
21 regional form of language
23 raised area of underwater land near the coast
25 having to do with cities
26 way of life
27 number of people per square mile
28 area outside a city where people live
32 movement into a country to live
33 long period with little or no rainfall
34 study of the earth and its features
36 river that flows into a larger river
38 part of a map that explains size
41 shows natural features
42 natural products used to make other things
46 travel for fun
47 seat of government
49 height of the land
50 wearing away of the earth
51 something that stands for a place, idea, etc.
52 place where a river empties into an ocean

REVIEWING TERMS PUZZLE ANSWERS

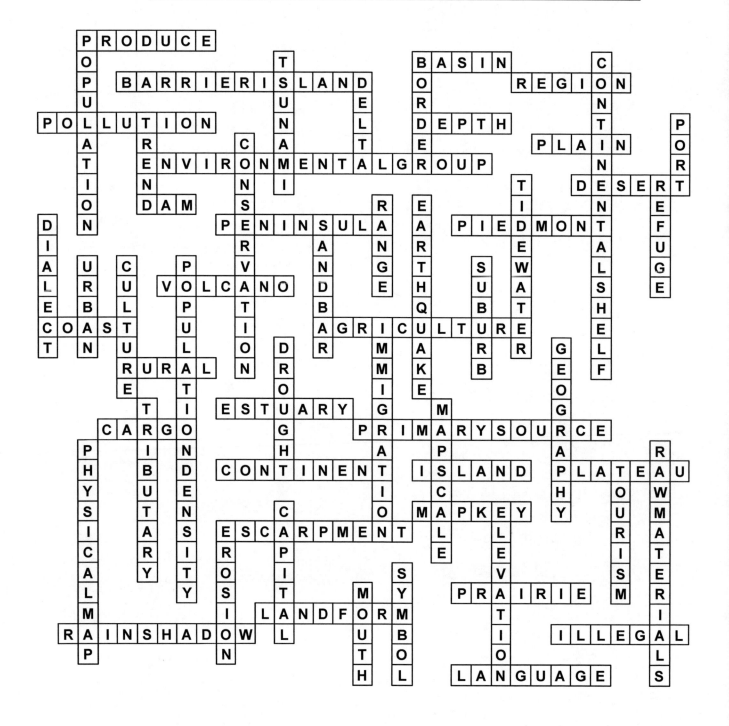

 **U.S. Regions (A)**

Matching - Put the letter of the answer in each blank:

1. ____ suburb
2. ____ coast
3. ____ delta
4. ____ border
5. ____ erosion
6. ____ illegal
7. ____ capital
8. ____ basin
9. ____ port
10. ____ produce

a. city that is a seat of government
b. triangle of land at the mouth of a river
c. place where ships load and unload
d. farm products
e. area outside a city where many people live
f. line which divides two countries or states
g. land that is next to an ocean
h. low land around a river
i. wearing down of the earth
j. against the law

Give an example of each:

11. region - _____
12. island - _____
13. landform - _____
14. coast - _____
15. continent - _____

Multiple Choice - Write the letter of the answer in each blank:

16. ____ All of these would be found in the Northeast, **EXCEPT**
    A. mountains.   C. islands.
    B. estuaries.   D. deserts.

17. ____ A physical map would **MOST LIKELY** show
    A. foods.   C. raw materials.
    B. oceans.   D. population density.

18. ____ Most people in the Southeast live in
    A. rural areas.   C. farming towns.
    B. urban areas.   D. the mountains.

19. ____ Which of these places would **CAUSE** a rain shadow?
    A. Mississippi River   C. Cascade Mountains
    B. the Great Lakes   D. the Empty Interior

Fully answer this question:

20. Explain at least two ways the geography of Alaska and Hawaii are different. _____

_____

_____

_____

_____

_____

_____

America's Tallest Mountain Peaks

Ranking	Name	State	Elevation (in feet)
1	Mt. McKinley	Alaska	20,320
2	Mt. St. Elias	Alaska	18,008
3	Mt. Foraker	Alaska	17,400
4	Mt. Bona	Alaska	16,500
5	Mt. Blackburn	Alaska	16,390
6	Mt. Sanford	Alaska	16,237
7	Mt. Vancouver	Alaska	15,979
8	South Buttress	Alaska	15,885
9	Mt. Churchill	Alaska	15,638
10	Mt. Fairweather	Alaska	15,300

21. ____ What can you say about Mt. McKinley based on the chart?
    A. America has many taller mountains.
    B. It is the highest mountain in the world.
    C. The peak is more than 30,000 feet tall.
    D. It is the tallest peak in the United States.

22. ____ "Mt." **MOST LIKELY** is
    A. a short way to write "mountain."
    B. a "peak" in the United States.
    C. always before a peak's name.
    D. an Alaskan word for "peak."

23. ____ What can you say is true based on the chart?
    A. Mt. Churchill is higher than Mt. Blackburn.
    B. No states besides Alaska have mountains.
    C. Alaska's mountain ranges are higher than other states'.
    D. Mt. McKinley is the highest mountain in North America.

California is home to some of the tallest trees in the world, giant redwoods. The northern coast of the state is perfect for them. The cool, damp air from the Pacific Ocean keeps the trees wet even in the summer.

Immense *redwoods grow from a seed no bigger than a tomato. They can live to be 2,000 years old and grow to more than 300 feet tall. That's as big as a 35-story building! The tallest living tree is 367½ feet. It is thought to be more than 1,000 years old.*

24. ____ The word "immense" in the reading means
    A. enormous.   C. ancient.
    B. interesting.   D. northern.

25. ____ Based on the reading, you could say that **ALL REDWOODS** are
    A. trees.   C. tall.
    B. old.   D. red.

 **U.S. Regions (B)**

Fill in the blanks with unit terms:

1. The _____ formed a triangle at the mouth of the river.
2. Many people live in the _____ outside of the city.
3. People who speak in a southern _____ often say "ya'all."
4. The United States is on the _____ of North America.
5. The _____ spewed lava and ash over the area.
6. The _____ shows mountains, rivers, and oceans.
7. The _____ flows into the Mississippi River.
8. Farm _____ includes fruits and vegetables.
9. The _____ was built to control flow of the river.
10. The _____ was filled with ships carrying all kinds of goods.

Give an example of each:

11. elevation - _____
12. pollution - _____
13. cargo - _____
14. symbol - _____
15. raw material - _____

Multiple Choice - Write the letter of the answer in each blank:

16. ____ Which would **MOST LIKELY** be seen in the Southwest?
    A. a volcano   C. an escarpment
    B. an estuary   D. a barrier island
17. ____ One problem faced by farmers in the Midwest is
    A. the price of farm products is going up.
    B. many small farmers are losing their land.
    C. their region is "America's breadbasket."
    D. land is shared between crops and animals.
18. ____ A physical map would probably include
    A. a rain shadow.   C. population density.
    B. raw materials.   D. a map key.
19. ____ Which of these places would **CAUSE** a rain shadow?
    A. Mississippi River   C. the Empty Interior
    B. Cascade Mountains   D. the Great Lakes

Fully answer this question:

20. Explain one way Alaska and Hawaii are alike and one way they are different.

 **U.S. Regions (C)**

Fill in the blanks with unit terms:

1. Products are to factories, as _____ is to farms.
2. Forest is to trees, as_____ is to grasslands.
3. Depth is to oceans, as _____ is to mountains.
4. Its spout is to a pitcher, as its _____ is to a river.
5. A wave is to tides, as a/an _____ is to an earthquake.
6. Language is to a country, as _____ is to a region.
7. Flood is to too much, as _____ is to not enough.
8. Rainforests are to huge amounts, as _____ are to hardly any.
9. Plateau is to high, as _____ is to low.
10. Wearing down is to shoe heels, as _____ is to the earth.

Give an example of each:

11. map scale - _____
12. peninsula - _____
13. volcano - _____
14. suburb - _____
15. tributary - _____

Multiple Choice - Write the letter of the answer in each blank:

16. _____ Texas, ___, Arizona, and ___ are in the Southwest Region.
    - A. Washington ... Wyoming
    - C. Louisiana ... Mississippi
    - B. New Mexico ... Oklahoma
    - D. California ... Montana
17. _____ All of these cities are part of the northeastern megalopolis **EXCEPT**
    - A. New York, NY
    - C. Baltimore, MD
    - B. Philadelphia, PA
    - D. Atlanta, GA
18. _____ Barrier islands
    - A. line the United States Pacific coast.
    - B. attract many tourists to swim and play.
    - C. change little over the course of time.
    - D. are rarely home to animal or plant life.
19. _____ Which of these places would be **CAUSED BY** a rain shadow?
    - A. Mississippi River
    - C. the Empty Interior
    - B. Cascade Mountains
    - D. the Great Lakes

Fully answer this question:

20. Compare and contrast the geography of Alaska and Hawaii. Include at least two ways the states are similar and two ways they differ.

Form A:

1. e
2. g
3. b
4. f
5. I
6. j
7. a
8. h
9. c
10. d

11. Northeast, Southwest, Rocky Mountain, Arctic, etc.
12. Hawaii, Oahu, Roanoke, Amelia Island, etc.
13. mountain, plateau, island, plain, etc.
14. Atlantic, Pacific, Gulf, east, west, etc.
15. North America, Europe, Africa, Asia, etc.
16. D
17. B
18. B
19. C
20. See differences in Form C answer.

Form B:

1. delta
2. suburb
3. dialect
4. continent
5. volcano
6. physical map
7. tributary
8. produce
9. dam
10. port

11. 16,000 feet, 500 meters, etc.
12. air, water, smog, litter, etc.
13. wood, oil, manufactured goods, produce, etc.
14. star, @, &, $\wedge$, $, etc.
15. wood, coal, water, gold, oil, etc.
16. C
17. B
18. D
19. B
20. See Form C answer.

Form C:

1. produce
2. prairie
3. elevation
4. mouth
5. tsunami
6. dialect
7. drought
8. deserts
9. plain
10. erosion

11. 1 inch = 200 miles, etc.
12. Baja, South Korea, Yucatan, etc.
13. Mt. St. Helens, Kilauea, Vesuvius, etc.
14. any suburb (not a major city)
15. Missouri River, Ohio River, Arkansas River, etc.
16. B
17. D
18. B
19. C
20. Similarities include: both are in the Ring of Fire, the Western Region, and both have mountains. Differences include: Hawaii is an island while Alaska is attached to North America; Hawaii has a warm climate while Alaska's is cold; Alaska is oil rich but Hawaii is rich in agriculture; etc.

Skills (for Forms A – C):

21. D
22. A
23. C
24. A
25. A

RESOURCES

usa.usembassy.de/travel-regions.htm - "The Regions of the United States," About the U.S.A., U.S. Diplomatic Mission to Germany, 2008.

worldatlat.com/webimage/countrys/nalnd.htm - "North America," WorldAtlas.com, 2008.

www.sierraclub.org/ecoregions/atlantic.asp - "Atlantic Coast Ecoregion," Sierra Club, 2008.

www.epa.gov/nep/about1.htm - "About Estuaries," National Estuary Program, U.S. Environmental Protection Agency, 2008.

www.americaslibrary.gov/cgi-bin/page.cgi/es/md/crab_1 - "Cracking Crabs in Maryland," Americas Story, The Library of Congress, 2008.

www.dnr.sc.gov/marine/pub/seascience/bluecrab.html - "Blue Crabs," Sea Science, Marine Resources Division South Carolina Department of Natural Resources, 2008.

www.gma.org/lobsters/ - "Lobsters," Gulf of Maine Research Institute, 1999.

www.umesc.usgs.gov/umesc_about/about_umrs.html - "About the Upper Mississippi River System," Upper Midwest Environmental Sciences Center, 2008.

www.nps.gov/guis/ - "Islands," Gulf Island National Seashore, 2008.

vaiden.net/convert.html - Collins, Ron, "Southern Dialect Converter," 2007.

money.cnn.com/galleries/2007/real_estate/0703/gallery.fastest_growing_counties/ - "Fastest Growing Counties," CNN MONEY.com, Cable News Network, 2008.

www.usatoday.com/news/nation/2004-04-08-loudon-growth_x.htm - Copeland, Larry, "Fastest-Growing Title More Headache than Honor," U.S.A. Today, Gannett, 2008.

www.enviroliteracy.org/article.php/92.html - Environmental Literacy Council, 2008.

etext.virginia.edu/toc/modeng/public/TwaLife.html - Twain, Mark, "Chapter 1," Life on the Mississippi, 1863, University of Virginia Library e-Text, 2008.

www.foodfirst.org/pubs/policybs/pb4.html - "On the Benefit of Small Farms," Food First, Institute for Food and Development Policy, 2008.

www.epa.gov/glnpo/ - "Great Lakes," Environmental Protection Agency, 2008.

www.greatlakesforever.org/ - Great Lakes Forever Biodiversity Project, 2008.

www.censusscope.org/us/rank_popl_growth.html - "Population Growth Rankings," Census Scope, Social Science Data Analysis Network, 2000.

www.lib.berkeley.edu/WRCA/WRC/wqp_issuessurvey.html - "Water Issues in the Southwest," University of California Center for Water Resources, 2008.

www.migrationinformation.org/Feature/display.cfm?id=407 - "The US-Mexico Border," Migration Information Source, Migration Policy Institute, 2006.

quake.usgs.gov/program/index.html - "Earthquake Hazards Program," USGS, 2008.

online.sfsu.edu/~leech/usgp/ - Geologic Provinces of the United States, San Francisco State University, 2008.

www.pacificislandtravel.com/hawaii/introduction.asp - "Hawaii," Pacific Island Travel, 2007.

www.npr.org/programs/morning/features/patc/hollywoodsign/index.html - "The Hollywood Sign," National Public Radio, 2002.

www.factmonster.com/ipka/A0001798.html - "Mountain Peaks in the United States Higher than 14,000 Feet," Fact Monster, Pearson Education Publishing, 2008.

www.nps.gov/redw/trees.html - "About the Trees," National Park Service, 2008.

i Think = Thematic Units

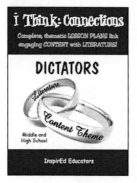  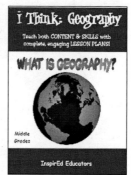

Some of our other **I Think** offerings include:

Series	Titles
I Think: Connections	Civilization
I Think: Connections	Democracy
I Think: Connections	Dictators
I Think: Connections	Ethnic Conflict
I Think: Connections	Imperialism
I Think: Connections	Indigenous People
I Think: U.S. History	Native Americans
I Think: U.S. History	Colonial America
I Think: U.S. History	American Revolution
I Think: U.S. History	The Civil War
I Think: U.S. History	Reconstruction Era
I Think: U.S. History	Modern America
I Think: Government	Civic Participation
I Think: Government	The Constitution
I Think: Government	The Executive Branch
I Think: Geography	What Is Geography?
I Think: World History	Ancient Greece
I Think: Reading & Writing	Poetry

We're adding more titles all the time.
Check our websites for current listings!

www.inspirededucators.com

www.inspiredhomeschoolers.com